Circle to God

LEE HOLSENBECK

WESTBOW
PRESS®
A DIVISION OF THOMAS NELSON
& ZONDERVAN

WestBow Press books may be ordered through booksellers or by contacting:

WestBow Press
A Division of Thomas Nelson & Zondervan
1663 Liberty Drive
Bloomington, IN 47403
www.westbowpress.com
1 (866) 928-1240

ISBN: 978-1-5127-9996-5 (sc)
ISBN: 978-1-5127-9998-9 (hc)
ISBN: 978-1-5127-9997-2 (e)

Library of Congress Control Number: 2017912458

Print information available on the last page.

WestBow Press rev. date: 9/8/2017

*To God Almighty, Maker of Heaven and Earth, from whom the
circle of life begins and with whom the circle of life ends*

Contents

chapter 1
Everything Is a Circle

A definition of the word "discovery" is "finding someone or something unexpectedly after searching." Isn't that what we all do many times throughout life or even often in the same day? We all search for meanings, explanations, and reasons for why things happen in the world and for why things do or do not happen to those we know and especially ourselves.

Although it may be hard to take, depending on where you stand or what your situation is, there is reasoning for why and how things happen. The difficulty for us to understand is that we cannot see the fullness of it. Some of us can split atoms, clone animals, walk across six-inch beams at a thousand feet, or fly planes faster than the speed of sound. But we still do not have the depth to understand the reasoning of things or events that seem to go against everything we think should be the right way, defy our interpretation of logical thought, and go exactly opposite of every expert prediction.

The reason that so many things just don't work out like we plan or go the way we wish is that it isn't about us. And when I say "us," I mean every person on the planet, the earth itself, and everything that everyone on this galactic sphere wants, needs, and desires. Yes, the rest of this book is going to sorely disappoint all of you steeped in the instant gratification, me-first society. The point of everything is to do one thing, to get everyone to turn, return, or run faster to God.

What you are going to find repeatedly throughout this book is that everything circles back to God or is God's effort to get people to cycle back to him. This should not be surprising, if you think about it. I mean, if you make or create something that benefits you and others, you more than likely hope you get some appreciation for it. Over and over, you can see that God has set everything in motion and, at some point, everything will point back to him. People will have cause to turn back to him yearly, weekly, or daily.

Many people at this point will scoff or flat-out disbelieve that the purposes of many things that occur in their or others' lives and on the planet have anything to do with God. And I agree with that. People do have free will, but if you are certain that God made the universe, then believing he set up the place so he is the central figure is not too far of a stretch. You might liken it to a casino, where the house is set up to win. I hope that comparison doesn't cost me in the future, but God has set things so he wins as well. The good news here is that, if God wins you, you do too. It seems to work the opposite way in a casino. Karma, good or bad luck, accidents, broken bones, life-threatening illness, and six billion people making choices every minute still make what happens on a daily basis, but God has set it all up so it points back to him.

Skepticism? Good. That's what I want. In this book, I intend to show over and over throughout the world, daily life, and the Bible itself that God is calling you back to him. Sometimes it's loud, other times you wouldn't notice, and in many cases, you missed it. But if you can find something in this book that you can relate to and find a way back to God or a closer relationship with him, then I have accomplished my mission.

Well, let's get started then. Many of us think or believe that the whole man-to-God relationship started with a guy named Adam, who is very unique in both biblical meaning and relation to each one of us. As we all know, Adam held high favor with God and communicated freely with him until he fell out of esteem with God by committing sin or putting his wants and needs ahead of what God wanted and needed for Adam.

I think many of us can relate to Adam, as we often feel that we are walking well with God's favor, or that God would be proud of our daily life if he were asked. Then through either our own doing or circumstances, we will stray from what God would find pleasing or living a positive or high quality of life to a period that might be considered selfish or even detrimental to ourselves as people. Or events give us pause that we deserved or have earned this or that as reward or revenge on the world that has denied or flat-out rejected our wants and needs for longer than we can take.

I do not doubt that Adam had similar thoughts, as he put himself ahead of God and cast the world into sin. I realize that we have put a lot on Adam. But if you were Adam and didn't know the consequences of what being the original sinner for the world would be, might you not have some selfish wants and desires? I imagine so. And what did Adam do? The same that you and I do when we fall short or put our needs ahead of what God would want. We seek redemption and forgiveness.

Isn't this what God wants from all of us? I think it is. So it is very reasonable to think he set things in motion so the very first of us would look to him for help. Everyone who follows should do the same in times of troubles, crises, or when things just aren't working out the way we had planned.

Now Adam also did a second thing or set it in motion. I do not know how there can possibly be good news that the world was cast into sin, but there is. If Adam had resisted temptation, desires, wants, or however you define his fall and raised a family that always followed God and their offspring did the same and so on, the Greeks would never have been able to write their tragedies, and there wouldn't be much to watch on television. But I digress.

No, if Adam hadn't succumbed to his desires, the entire world would have not been given or needed redemption in Jesus Christ. And what is redemption in Jesus Christ if you put it in broad terms and not the specifics of salvation for anyone who claims Christ as Lord and Savior? It is the ultimate call of God to have people return to him. "For Christ also suffered once for sins, the righteous for the unrighteous, to bring you to God." (1 Peter 3:18a)

I put forth that the entire time, starting with Adam, God knew people would get distracted with life, be treated wrongly, and face hardships. And from Genesis, God was the answer to help people deal with the problems in life, but they would need a stronger call to seek him, which came in Jesus Christ.

If we look throughout the Old Testament, we can see that its people have called upon God. It was not just Adam who had needs that might have been similar to those we have today, necessities that, after failures of our own or others to fulfill, we ask God to accomplish. It was the same repeatedly with the people in the Old Testament that God was called to fill their needs and desires. David sang this after being rescued from Saul, "In my distress I called to the LORD; I called out to my God. From his temple he heard my voice; my cry came to his ears." (2 Samuel 22:7)

And in the book of Jonah, we see that, even after he runs away from the Lord, he returns to him after being saved by God. "To the roots of the mountains I sank down; the earth beneath barred me in forever. But you, LORD my God, brought my life up from the pit." (Jonah 2:6)

So you see clearly that today, as in the Old Testament, it doesn't matter if we have turned away from God as Jonah did, have sought God in times of troubles as David did, or do not think to call on God except on Sunday mornings, as does much of the world today. It is still a seeking of God that he wishes for you, no matter where you are in life, in order for you to have a closer relationship with him.

It doesn't matter what makes us turn or return to God. He is not expecting or drawing lines in the sand for when a person should turn to him, as he doesn't have to. He knows all the lines you will cross in your life and when you will need him most. This same God put the solar system perfectly in place to hold life on Earth. He knew you before you were born and knows all of your days. He will always be there for those days when you need him most.

chapter 2
Your Life Is a Path to God

You may not know or believe it. I mean, how could you be on a path to God when you are sitting in traffic for two hours on a rain-soaked Thursday night? How could you be on a track to God when you just broke your hip and it's going to take six months to recover, if you do at all? You definitely can't be on a route to God if you were just let go from a job you planned on retiring from or if you're in an abusive relationship, but I submit you are.

The part that most people miss in situations like these or other circumstances in life, be they good or bad, is that the pathway is not yours. It is God's. And God has many roads to him. Some are expressways, others have oncoming traffic, and a few have stoplights, but there are still many roads to him in our lives.

Then there is the opposite end of the spectrum where everything is rolling right along and going according to plans or even better than planned. You're getting your third promotion in three years, the man or woman in your life is happy to have you and lets you know it regularly, or you just don't have a complaint. Yes, there are many up and downs in life, sometimes more rises and occasionally more falls, but they are still full of off-ramps or even dead ends where you are going to run right into God. You might remember this parable from Matthew 13:24–30,

Jesus told them another parable: "The kingdom of heaven is like a man who sowed good seed in his field. But while everyone was sleeping, his enemy came and sowed weeds among the wheat, and went away. When the wheat sprouted and formed heads, then the weeds also appeared. The owner's servants came to him and said, 'Sir, didn't you sow good seed in your field? Where then did the weeds come from?'

'An enemy did this,' he replied.

The servants asked him, 'Do you want us to go and pull them up?'

'No,' he answered, 'because while you are pulling the weeds, you may uproot the wheat with them. Let both grow together until the harvest. At that time I will tell the harvesters: First collect the weeds and tie them in bundles to be burned; then gather the wheat and bring it into my barn.'"

While people are busy with their lives, both good and bad things are going to happen, but throughout their existence, there will be paths leading them to God. What people do not realize, because they are not God, is that he is preparing them to have a relationship with him. The reason this seems to happen only in moments and not continually is that, as your life changes day by day and sometimes minute by minute, there are only certain moments when you are in the right frame of mind or are willing to listen to what God is trying to tell you.

What happens much like the parable above is that you too will grow weeds during the daily course of your life from relationships, careers, wants, desires, and even vacations that will become entangled with the wheat that God is harvesting in your life to bring you and others that you know or have influence on closer to him. God knows this and will gather the wheat of your life to him when you are ready. "When he has brought out all his own, he goes on ahead of them, and his sheep follow him because they know his voice." (John 10:4)

What we as people do not understand, because we are not all-knowing and all-seeing as God is, is that our heavenly Father is already ahead of us. It may be two miles ahead of us with a sign in lights that says, "Turn here for a joyful experience." Or it may be twenty miles ahead of us, and we cannot even seem to see or feel God's presence. Or it might just be a few steps to where his presence overwhelms us.

But he is there and has been in that spot. We may not notice it when we get to where God has been or wants us to be, as it is not his nature to reveal everything to man, much like many parents have told their children, "It's for your own good," without taking the time to explain why because they know from experience what the best thing to do is. So does God.

What is happening is "prevenience," where God has already gone ahead and put things in motion so that, when we get to places in life, he has already set a path to bring us into a closer relationship with him or made a roadblock to keep us from a route that will lead away from him. It is always hard to see that you are walking a track to God when you are traversing it, as there are always twists and turns in life that you are sure that God wouldn't have made you go through if he had your best interests in mind. And there may be several stops and periods where you have to wait and wait and wait until you can move to a better place in life. There may even be—and in many cases there are—periods of pain and discomfort that you have to go through before you get to a better place, but if you look back, you may see that every twist, turn, wait, and stop happened at exactly the right time to get you to a closer relationship with God, which is what he wanted in the first place.

You can see the same throughout the Bible, where people have taken many twists and turns through their days, and it always leads back to God's plan for their lives. Some of the routes they walked to get to God's plan for them cost them very little, but in many cases throughout the Bible, it cost them everything they knew.

In Genesis, Joseph was sold into slavery by his own brothers and imprisoned, but he ended up ruling all of Egypt. The path that God had started Joseph on literally cost him everything he knew: his family, his birthright, his land, and anything he might inherit from his family. At any point, Joseph could have doubted God or doubted where his Father was guiding him, but he did not. Even while imprisoned, Joseph was on God's path. "But while Joseph was there in the prison, the LORD was with him; he showed him kindness and granted him favor in the eyes of the prison warden." (Genesis 39:20–21)

Joseph focused on following the path that God had set before him and listening to his heavenly Father through his dreams, and God favored Joseph. Even after Joseph becomes ruler of Egypt and his own brothers who sold him into slavery confront him, he chooses not to condemn them and instead decides to praise God for what he has allowed Joseph to accomplish.

> Joseph said to his brothers, "I am Joseph! Is my father still living?" But his brothers were not able to answer him, because they were terrified at his presence. Then Joseph said to his brothers, "Come close to me." When they had done so, he said, "I am your brother Joseph, the one you sold into Egypt! And now, do not be distressed and do not be angry with yourselves for selling me here, because it was to save lives that God sent me ahead of you. For two years now there has been famine in the land, and for the next five years there will be no plowing and reaping. But God sent me ahead of you to preserve for you a remnant on earth and to save your lives by a great deliverance. So then,

it was not you who sent me here, but God. He made me father to Pharaoh, lord of his entire household and ruler of all Egypt. Now hurry back to my father and say to him, 'This is what your son Joseph says: God has made me lord of all Egypt. Come down to me; don't delay.'" (Genesis 45:3–9)

Joseph lays no blame on his brothers who acted completely selfishly and were very jealous of the attention their natural father seemed to show Joseph. To sell him into slavery might have been a part of God's plan but was completely their doing. Yet Joseph does not take one moment to scold them for betraying their own flesh and blood. Instead he shows them that their action was a part of a much bigger plan of God's. Not only would a plan give Joseph a much greater life than he could ever imagine, it also would save lives throughout the entire nation of Egypt, including his own brothers who betrayed him.

Now we cannot all become rulers of a country or save scores of people from problems they have in life, but we can all have an impact if we can follow the path that God sets before us. I know most of us cannot see we are walking it or even if we are near it, but it is there, and it just may take us longer to find in today's world of constant distraction by cell phones, television, and the Internet.

What we fail to understand here is that God sees and knows all of the possible paths we could take. We do not comprehend this because, for most of us, we usually only see the path right in front of us and are usually too busy with families, work, bills, the daily responsibilities of life, and the even greater complexities that we encounter engaging, joining, and even avoiding other people with the responsibilities of their lives. Most people do not gain the wisdom and experience to see that, in almost every situation, there were many paths to take until later in their lives.

However, God has infinite wisdom and knows every path in life we can take, and that is why he seems to be waiting for us at just the right time to help us take the trail that will lead back to him. You see, God has this advantage as he knew us in eternity. He knew us before birth, and his knowledge preceded us. And this is how he is able to meet us, no matter where we find ourselves. His knowledge of us is encyclopedic, utterly honest, complete, and compassionate.

This is how God can be there when you least expect it. He has been there for all time and certainly will be there at the moment you are needing him most. You can see now that God has known us since the beginning and will know us until the end as he created the beginning and end of all things.

God does not need to get to know us any better since he knew us from before our own beginnings and before we were born. This is why our lives are a circle—or a series of circles—to God. Through the journeys of our lives, we come to know God and where he and his plans for our lives are to be revealed to us.

Now let us begin to look at some of life's experiences that affect or have impacted all of us and see that God is working to help us through them, meet us in those experiences, and be there with us.

chapter 3
Finding God in Life's Disappointments

There's one thing for certain in life: it will be full of disappointments, which come in all shapes and colors. You may be disappointed in your past, current, or future circumstance. You may be disappointed in others, or you can even be dissatisfied in yourself.

Trust me. These disappointments occur to all people and on a daily basis and have happened throughout time. Even Moses had disappointments. "Moses returned to the LORD and said, 'Why, LORD, why have you brought trouble on this people? Is this why you sent me? Ever since I went to Pharaoh to speak in your name, he has brought trouble on this people, and you have not rescued your people at all.'" (Exodus 5:22–23)

In this case, Moses was disappointed with God himself, but as we can see in the scriptures, God was allowing Moses to go through this period of dissatisfaction in order to deliver his people to their rightful land.

> "Go, assemble the elders of Israel and say to them, 'The LORD, the God of your fathers—the God of Abraham, Isaac, and Jacob—appeared to me and said: I have watched over you and have seen what has been done to you in Egypt. And I have promised to bring you up out of your misery in Egypt into the land of

the Canaanites, Hittites, Amorites, Perizzites, Hivites and Jebusites—a land flowing with milk and honey.'" (Exodus 3:16–17)

If you read through Exodus, you will find that there were many disappointments and hardships the people of Israel endured, but these led to God and Israel becoming his people. It is the same for us as we encounter disappointment. We may be discouraged or even turn away from God, but he is not looking for that. During some of the greatest disappointments we will face, God is looking for us to turn to him.

In the book of Esther, we can see the disappointment of Esther having to face the possibility of giving up her title as queen and probably even her own life to save her people.

> When Esther's words were reported to Mordecai, he sent back this answer: "Do not think that because you are in the king's house you alone of all the Jews will escape. For if you remain silent at this time, relief and deliverance for the Jews will arise from another place, but you and your father's family will perish. And who knows but that you have come to your royal position for such a time as this?" Then Esther sent this reply to Mordecai: "Go, gather together all the Jews who are in Susa, and fast for me. Do not eat or drink for three days, night or day. I and my maids will fast as you do. When this is done, I will go to the king, even though it is against the law. And if I perish, I perish." (Esther 4:12–16)

Now most of us will not face disappointments as great as Moses did with God himself or as threatening to you as they were to Esther's position in life and threats to her ancestry, but when we face setbacks, they can be just as personal to us as they were likely to be to Moses and Esther. In both of their cases, God was bringing them to rely on him, which led to better lives for their people.

What happens in today's world where some of us (especially in the United States) have life so easy that even the slightest struggles can turn us into the darkest of moods, maybe bordering on socially acceptable depression, is that we expect everything to come up roses. This is even in cases of faithful Christians who expect those roses to be prize winners because they go to church.

However, there will be setbacks in daily life for all of us, which are opportunities for us to look to God for support and comfort instead of relying on a mood-altering outing, a pint of ice cream, drug (prescription or otherwise), and/or pleasures that are just temporary fixes or Band-Aids over the real solution, which is to look to God and the Bible for answers for the problems you are facing.

A large issue for so many people today (and some might even say it is a stumbling block that limits people's ability to seek God in this modern era) is that we are addicted to instant answers. In this information age where we can find any material we need for anything we desire or need, it is almost impossible to wait for something to be provided to us, and asking more than once for an item is almost unheard of today.

But this is where the omnipotence of God wins out over a Google search as he knows where you have been, where you are now, and what is best for your future. God has been planning the paths of the lives of people who follow him all the way back to Moses and Esther and keeping them on the route that was best for them, their lives, and the lives of their people. And he will do the same for you if you will follow him and trust in him.

We can see one of the best examples of man's attempts to validate his circumstances and his peers justifying occurrences in his life in the book of Job. Job suffers much pain and disappointment in his life but expects everything to go well and comes up with no reason why things started going wrong, as he could not find anything to blame on himself. "Although I am blameless, I have no concern for myself; I despise my own life. It is all the same; that is why I say, 'He destroys both the blameless and the wicked." (Job 9:21–22)

Job can find no reason why the suffering he has to endure has fallen on him. As a righteous man, he should have no problems. I am sure we all feel like this at certain times or periods of our lives. We seem to be swimming through life nicely and then start encountering a series of falls, setbacks, and even catastrophes, sometimes all in the same month.

And just like Job, we cannot figure out why. We have not done anything that we can imagine would set God off to seek vengeance against us and do not remember the last time that we could be accused of spreading bad karma. But here we are, stuck in quicksand, and everything we grab at to try to get out and get back on solid footing comes loose, and we sink a little further.

And it is not just ourselves who cannot understand how sufferings come to affect us when we feel undeserving of it. Those around us also may wonder why you are having all these troubles. I am sure we all know of a person (or persons) who are of the highest character or always a joy for everyone to be around. In the midst of a very positive path in life, they are hit by a freight train that affects them like some devastating disease or a close relationship that tears apart their life. Job's friends, Eliphaz, Bildad, and Zophar saw the same thing for Job and figured that the trials he had encountered must have been of his own doing. "Consider now: Who, being innocent, has ever perished? Where were the upright ever destroyed? As I have observed, those who plow evil and those who sow trouble reap it." (Job 4:7–8)

Finally Job challenges even God himself as to why such a righteous man as himself could be afflicted with so many problems, and questions as to what makes God so great if he can let so many misgivings affect such a faithful person. I'm sure many of us have done this as well.

We look at ourselves or others we know or know of and wonder how an omnipotent God could allow so many hardships to fall upon us when so many others are more deserving of the poor fortunes we have inherited. But I suspect that God would refer us to the story of Job. "What is the way to the abode of light? And where does darkness reside? Can you take them to their places? Do you know the paths to their dwellings? Surely you know, for you were already born! You have lived so many years!" (Job 38:19–21)

You see, when we question God who has created light and hung billions of planets in perfect orbits, when life is not going according to our plans, we just have no idea who we are talking to. When having the ability of the kind of power to keep the entire universe in order, the wisdom and justice of God over you is faultless. Once we come to this realization of just how big God is, we can see how little our problems are to him and to trust in him that he will be there when the time comes for our needs. But it will be on his timetable and not our own, as we do not have the ability to see time as God does.

We can refer to Hebrews 11:1 that we should see God as whom we should put our faith in, "Now faith is confidence in what we hope for and assurance about what we do not see." And throughout Hebrews 11 is a list of people who lived through very hard times in their lives and went through many trials, some even by God himself, but these people did not lose their faith that their heavenly Father would see them through. And in each case, their lives contributed more than they ever could have imagined as they sought to be part of God's plan and not their own.

In the story of Cain and Abel, Cain brought a sacrifice to God of his own work and not of faith in God, while Abel brought a sacrifice to God from the faith he had in God.

> Now Abel kept flocks, and Cain worked the soil. In
> the course of time Cain brought some of the fruits

of the soil as an offering to the LORD. And Abel also brought an offering—fat portions from some of the firstborn of his flock. The LORD looked with favor on Abel and his offering, but on Cain and his offering he did not look with favor. So Cain was very angry, and his face was downcast. Then the LORD said to Cain, "Why are you angry? Why is your face downcast? If you do what is right, will you not be accepted?" (Genesis 4:2–7a)

God was telling Cain to seek what pleases God and not himself, but Cain could not do that. So he instead let the sin of jealousy of the favor God had for his brother Abel, who sought God in his labor, end in him killing his brother.

Now you would think that there was no way any good came out of this for Abel, someone who sought to please God. It ended up costing him his own life. I mean, why would we want to please God if it's going to cost us our own lives? It may be hard to relate to Cain and Abel, but I am sure we all know of at least one story of a Christian missionary or someone who calls themself a believer in Christ who has been brutally attacked or killed, and he or she was doing what was pleasing to God, just like Abel. What we are not observing here is what we cannot see, and only God can as he has a knowledge of time and the lives of people like no person can because he is God. Here we can see that, even though Abel died by the hand of someone refusing to seek God, he was rewarded even after his death by his seeking of God. "By faith Abel brought God a better offering than Cain did. By faith he was commended as righteous, when God spoke well of his offerings. And by faith Abel still speaks, even though he is dead." (Hebrews 11:4)

That's a little bit of a brutal example of how a person might have trials in life, but in the end, it can still be a part of the plan God has for them. The story of Abraham, one so many people know of and who is regarded as the father of the Jewish nation, had to leave his home at seventy-five years old to establish the Jewish nation and had his faith further tested by God in committing to sacrifice his own son.

I do not think the messages we hear from God are so clear today, but Abraham didn't have the constant barrage of distractions we have today. If Abraham had an iPhone and television with five hundred channels, just think what the world could have missed.

> "I will surely bless you and make your descendants as numerous as the stars in the sky and as the sand on the seashore. Your descendants will take possession of the cities of their enemies, and through your offspring all nations on earth will be blessed, because you have obeyed me." (Genesis 22:17–18)

Finally we have Moses, someone who was tried his entire life for his faith from his very birth, but at no point did Moses not do what God had planned for his life.

> By faith Moses, when he had grown up, refused to be known as the son of Pharaoh's daughter. He chose to be mistreated along with the people of God rather than to enjoy the fleeting pleasures of sin. He regarded disgrace for the sake of Christ as of greater value than the treasures of Egypt, because he was looking ahead to his reward. By faith he left Egypt, not fearing the king's anger; he persevered because he saw him who is invisible. By faith he kept the Passover and the application of blood, so that the destroyer of the firstborn would not touch the firstborn of Israel. (Hebrews 11:24–28)

As we can see from Abel to Abraham to Moses, choosing to seek God's plan for your life is not an easy path and may take you places you would not choose to go. It may even cost you your life, but if you will have faith in him and his plan for your life, you just may be amazed at what you will accomplish. I know it may be hard to see or pick out God's plan for your life or even that he has a plan for your life. You may be one of thousands on the local freeway, making the daily grind to work, or one of hundreds of thousands in some city, wondering just how he is going to pick you out amongst the crowd and turn your life around.

Well, may I refer you to the apostle Paul? I know most of us know about the road to Damascus where Paul encounters the presence of Christ and is blinded but converted from being a persecutor of followers of Christ to one of Christ's greatest advocates.

However, what many of us may not remember is that the same Paul, named Saul at that point, was just a face in the crowd as Stephen was stoned to death for his testament to the Lord. "At this they covered their ears and, yelling at the top of their voices, they all rushed at him, dragged him out of the city and began to stone him. Meanwhile, the witnesses laid their coats at the feet of a young man named Saul." (Acts 7:57–58)

Even though Paul was just a face in the crowd then, God picked him out to do some of the greatest things in the history of Christianity. Who is to say that you haven't been picked and just don't know it yet? It seems that Paul figured this out, "And we know that in all things God works for the good of those who love him, who have been called according to his purpose." (Romans 8:28)

If you would have told Paul at the time that Stephen was being stoned that he was going to stop persecuting Christians in the near future, and that he would spend the rest of his life preaching about Christ, and he would be the sole instrument to bring Gentiles to be believers in Christ in the early church, he may have started throwing stones at you and not let up until you were dead or at least unconscious.

So how can you stand with feet firmly planted in cement and refuse to listen for God and seek him in the scriptures to find out what he has planned for your life when everything you have tried and are trying has resulted in banging your head against that same concrete that you have poured around your feet?

We need only to look to the words of God himself to see he is there with us in the tough times and looking to help us in times we struggle. "So do not fear, for I am with you; do not be dismayed, for I am your God, I will strengthen you and help you; I will uphold you with my righteous right hand." (Isaiah 41:10)

If this is the same God that has placed the earth perfectly so it would give us the air we breathe and be just far enough from the sun so it grows enough food to feed the billions of people and hundreds of billions of animals each year without fail, then how can he not also be there to help you in your time of need? Of course, the part that confuses, saddens, and angers us is that we believe that we know when we are in a time of need and expect God to be there. But this is why he is God and we are merely people whose reference point is usually ourselves. It is very hard for most of us to see anything or perceive the meaning of why something is happening to us.

And it is even more difficult for us to see things from a viewpoint other than our own, but this is why we must always seek God. He can perceive all of the decisions we could make and everything that could happen to us depending on what choice we make. He can even see the consequences of those decisions that we could never have imagined and even view things that are going to happen to us because of others' actions or inactions. When you have created light, you can see the time corresponding to that light, and this is why we should lean hard on God and seek him throughout all of our lives.

I know it is hard to see that we should trust in God when we are going through a difficult time and cannot even remember the last time that something went right for us, but again we are looking at our circumstances through our lenses and not God's. We can see a prime example in Jeremiah 29 of a people in the Bible who must give up years and years of the lives they are living for the promise of a better life from God.

In Jeremiah 29, God addresses his people who have been exiled from Jerusalem and must live in captivity in the pagan city of Babylon for many years until he delivers them back to Jerusalem. These people have been uprooted from their homeland and many of their friends and family, and they are now subject to live under the rule of a king that could result in anything from a more difficult daily life to an existence that may be threatened if the king decides or is presented with reason to not trust or harbor ill will against the people of Jerusalem.

I know that you may have had a long time or even years where life has been a struggle for you, but these people were exiled for seventy years, an entire lifetime for some of them, of trying times and separation from what they knew and loved. Yet knowing that it would be so long, God says to seek him.

> "For I know the plans I have for you," declares the LORD, "plans to prosper you and not to harm you, plans to give you hope and a future. Then you will call on me and come and pray to me, and I will listen to you. You will seek me and find me when you seek me with all your heart." (Jeremiah 29:11–13)

Two things here show that God should be the only one that we should turn to in times of difficulty in our lives. "For I know the plans I have for you" is a testament to the omnipotent God that we all live under, and even while every road we take or decision we make seems to be bad, God has plans for your life, and they are good, specifically "plans to prosper you and not to harm you, plans to give you hope and a future."

Some of us may have had a very rough childhood where we were a nuisance to our parents at best, and the very parents that gave birth to us may have abused others of us. But that is not the kind of parent God is. He has plans for good things for our lives, to give us "hope and a future." This is the kind of God we live and serve, someone that seeks the best for our lives according to his plans for our life. This is the hard part for most of us, that is, we cannot find God's plan for our lives, which brings me to the second part of the quote from Jeremiah 29, "You will seek me and find me when you seek me with all your heart."

For most of us, we do not seek God with all of our heart. Instead we wish to seek God according to our needs and on our timetable, but as we can clearly see in Jeremiah 29, this is not the way that God works in our lives. He is working in our lives according to his timetable for us, and this is set up to bring us into a closer relationship with him.

If the exiles from Jerusalem could have just spent a year in captivity in Babylon and then began daily prayers to God until he relented and made it possible for them to go back to their homeland of Jerusalem, don't you think they would have done so?

I certainly do, but that is not what God knew was best for them. They wouldn't have sought God with everything they had if the ends could be so easily had, and this is why God was so clear in what it would take to reach him with his words, "You will seek me and find me when you seek me with all your heart."

It is the same with us. If we do not seek God with everything we have, then God is not going to listen and answer. This is most likely why so many prayers go unanswered today. With a culture that assaults our senses nearly nonstop, seeking anything with all of our heart is a very difficult task, but this is what God is asking of us, to seek him fully and without limits.

You may hesitate to do that. I mean it is very unusual for us to give ourselves wholly to one thing as the governing force in our lives.

So many of us rely on so many different things from parents, spouses, friends, coworkers, authority figures, or highly regarded resources or behavioral methods. Some of us even rely partly or wholly on drugs, prescribed or otherwise, when none of that can hold a candle to God, as can be seen in Isaiah 40:28–31,

> Do you not know? Have you not heard? The LORD is the everlasting God, the Creator of the ends of the earth. He will not grow tired or weary, and his understanding no one can fathom. He gives strength to the weary and increases the power of the weak. Even youths grow tired and weary, and young men stumble and fall; but those who hope in the LORD will renew their strength. They will soar on wings like eagles; they will run and not grow weary, they will walk and not be faint.

What is happening in Isaiah is that God has come to give comfort to the oppressed and suffering people of Israel. After Nebuchadnezzar conquered and destroyed Jerusalem, he held its people captive for seventy years, and the people of Israel were greatly distressed at what had become of the once great Jerusalem, as can be seen in Lamentations, "How deserted lies the city, once so full of people! How like a widow is she, who once was great among the nations!" (Lamentations 1:1)

Despite the decades of oppression by Nebuchadnezzar over the people of Israel, God tells them that he will uplift them as long as they keep their hope in him. Some of these people literally spent their whole lives living under oppression. I suppose the best we could relate to it would be to think of someone who had spent nearly his or her entire life in prison for being wrongly accused. You would never know when or if you would be exonerated, but once you were, you would feel like a huge weight had been taken off your back. Imagine how tough it was for those people, living in captivity and subject to all sorts of oppressive behavior from their Babylonian captors for years and years to trust that God was working to give them better lives and deliver on his promises to them. It might seem like whatever struggles you have gone through are lasting years, but I think the people of Jerusalem may have won the medal of enduring suffering. I believe you can trust that the same words God gave to the people of Israel apply to you and your life.

As God told the people of Israel, "Those who hope in the Lord will renew their strength," so it will be the same in your life. And just as you do, question why something is happening to you and why you are suffering. The same was asked by the people of Jerusalem in Lamentations. I'm sure that if God were to speak to you, he would refer you to Isaiah and to the same words he spoke to the people of Jerusalem, "The Lord is the everlasting God, the Creator of the ends of the earth. He will not grow tired or weary, and his understanding no one can fathom."

Neither you nor I can greater understand why we may be suffering through something, and we cannot come up with one idea why we deserve it than the people of Jerusalem did. But this is why he is God. We are merely people who desire to seek him and do what is pleasing in God's eyes, and if we pin our hopes upon God, we "will soar on wings like eagles."

I know it is difficult to believe that God does indeed desire for the best in each of us. I mean, over a billion people are living in China alone. How can God be concerned with your life when he is dealing with billions and billions of people daily who are facing greater needs than yours? They may be facing life-and-death decisions that affect themselves or others. They may be considering life-altering choices that will impact the rest of their lives, or some may just be looking to God and praying to him over something as easy as which cat to get from the adoption center. How can your needs find their way to God in the midst of all of that?

And I would reply to you that you are putting limits on God, who is limitless! We can look to the words from Jesus himself on how valuable each of us is to God, "Are not two sparrows sold for a penny? Yet not one of them will fall to the ground outside your Father's care. And even the very hairs of your head are all numbered. So don't be afraid; you are worth more than many sparrows." (Matthew 10:29–31)

Do you know that the estimate of the world's bird population is so great that there isn't even an estimate? It's a range, and the estimated number of the world's bird population is between 200 and 400 billion birds. You would think, when you can't even make an estimate within 100 billion, the surveyors of the world's bird populations really have no idea. But they know it's at least 200 billion birds while there are only around 7 billion people on the planet, and God knows if one of those 200 billion (or more) birds falls to the ground. This is a great example of what I mean when I say that God is limitless. And if you believe that he is not working in your life, then you are limiting God.

You should not limit God. Instead you should do what the people of Jerusalem did during the time of Isaiah and appoint watchmen for God. You see, in Isaiah's time, watchmen were often posted on the city's walls to look out or watch for approaching enemies, but they could also be on the watch for messengers who were bringing good news to the city. If they fell asleep while on watch, enemies could take the city, or good tidings could be delayed.

In a similar manner, the people of Israel are supposed to be on watch, not only against those who would threaten Jerusalem, but also for the Lord himself, who has promised to bless his people as we can see in Isaiah 62, "I have posted watchmen on your walls, Jerusalem; they will never be silent day or night. You who call on the LORD, give yourselves no rest, and give him no rest till he establishes Jerusalem and makes her the praise of the earth." (Isaiah 62:6–7)

God is essentially saying here to the people of Jerusalem to continually seek God until he fulfills his promises and makes Jerusalem the "praise of the earth." God has already told them that he will bring this blessing to Jerusalem, but he still wants the people to call on him regularly. He seeks the same for you and me. He wants us to be on watch for him. Even if it seems as if what we ask of God is being given, God still desires us to regularly seek him and have a relationship with him, but not just for the moment when we need him or when we are lonely. No, he is seeking a relationship for our entire life.

So let's begin with this suggestion that, no matter how strong we feel our relationship with God is now, we consider it a life relationship. All the other problems are important but will seem small over time if we consider that our biggest life partnership should be with God.

So let's consider that.

chapter 4
Trusting in God

Well, now that we have decided that the truly big question, after seeing example after example in the previous chapter of God working through our lives and lives of those in the Bible, is "Are you going to trust God with your life?"

Do not worry. There will be plenty of time to see where God has been there and will be there for you for the times in your life, but we really need to first consider if we are going to cede that kind of authority at all and if we are going to have a real relationship with God.

What may come as a surprise to many of us is that we never had that authority over our own life in the first place. Yes, many will say that God has no authority over them, and they are in charge of every decision they make. They'll tell you they could curse, steal, or sleep with the neighbor's wife and nothing is going to happen to them. If they do not get caught, that is probably true, but that is not what I am talking about. Deciding to do those things or choosing to do or not do almost anything is free will.

This is not the same as trusting God with having authority over your life, and something that all those who think they are in charge fail to grasp is that they were never in charge of their lives anyway. I'd suggest to you not to tell them that, or you are likely to hear some cursing, along with some denial and possible name-calling.

No, what I am talking about is coming to the realization that God is the great "I AM" and he has authority over all things, and seeking to trust in him to lead your life is the best decision you will ever make, as every choice you make or path you will choose will be one that God has already provided.

We can refer again to Jeremiah 29 to show that, just as God was working through a time of great difficulty and oppression of the exiles who lived in captivity in Babylon, he is working in your life. "For I know the plans I have for you," declares the LORD, "plans to prosper you and not to harm you, plans to give you hope and a future." (Jeremiah 29:11)

God was not some passive heavenly Father that set the world in motion and sat back while the exiles endured many hardships. No, he was working the whole time to give them a better future than they ever could have imagined, and the same plans for their "hope and a future" are plans that he has for your life. If God were predisposed to bring about better times for the exiles and he is a being of reason and logic, which according to all accounts in the Bible, he is. Then it follows that God would have plans for a "hope and future" for people of today, just as much or more than the exiles since the people of today live under the new covenant. As we can see in Ephesians, "In him we were also chosen, having been predestined according to the plan of him who works out everything in conformity with the purpose of his will." (Ephesians 1:11)

If you can accept that God had planned for the exiles to go through the trials and tribulations that they did while living in captivity and he had also intended to bring them through those experiences to an even better life than they could have imagined, then it is not hard to comprehend, as you can see in the statement above, that God had already set things up so you would be part of his plans many generations before you were even born.

This is what Paul is saying in Ephesians 1:11 in that we were "predestined." The people of today can choose to follow God's plan through Jesus Christ that was put in place before the first man walked the earth. And if God has had a plan in place for all the people of today to come to him in their lives, then he certainly is going to have multiple paths throughout your life to lead you back to him.

What we need to understand as we learn to trust that God has our best interests in mind and is working to give each of us a prosperous future is that he is still God and we are just people. There is just no way that we can comprehend everything God is doing in our lives while at the same time fulfilling his plans as God. We can best see this in Isaiah 55:8–11,

> "For my thoughts are not your thoughts, neither are your ways my ways," declares the LORD. "As the heavens are higher than the earth, so are my ways higher than your ways and my thoughts than your thoughts. As the rain and the snow come down from heaven, and do not return to it without watering the earth and making it bud and flourish, so that it yields seed for the sower and bread for the eater, so is my word that goes out from my mouth: It will not return to me empty, but will accomplish what I desire and achieve the purpose for which I sent it."

As you can see in Isaiah 55:8–11, the ways of the Lord are not always the same that you and I are striving for or experiencing. In fact, we may even be hindering what God has planned and think we are doing something that is entirely focused on a godly life and may still have struggles or difficulty. And this is because we are still going against God's plan for us, and eventually he will win because what God designs "shall prosper in the thing for which I sent it."

This flies in the face of the culture today. Most people view their lives contrary to the first part of Hebrews 2:8, "In putting everything under them, God left nothing that is not subject to them. Yet at present we do not see everything subject to them."

The first part, "putting everything under them, God left nothing that is not subject to them," seems to work just fine for most, if not all, of us. Most of us want to know the feeling of control over everything in our lives, and oftentimes it looks like we have that. But this is where God separates himself from us. He can see the things in our lives, past and present, that may be taking control of our lives, and this makes seeking God as a guide in our lives the best decision we could ever make.

This is where the term used previously, "prevenience," comes into focus. God has already been everywhere you might go and has currently been working to involve you as part of his plans, and seeking him and then following his design for your life can lead you to a greater life than you could ever imagine. You can see this in John 10:4, "When he has brought out all his own, he goes on ahead of them, and his sheep follow him because they know his voice."

In the same sense that John is referring to Jesus, we can refer to God. God has put forth all of his efforts to create heaven and earth and each of our lives, and he has done this long before any of us came about. Seeking and listening for God in our lives is the natural state of men and women. And luckily for us, it is also the natural state for God.

God desires for us to seek him out. The catch is that he is not waiting for us to seek him during the Sunday morning call to worship before the choir starts or when you see the oncoming car skidding into your lane on a wet road, although he hopes you do seek him in those times. He is really wanting you to seek him constantly. "I love those who love me, and those who seek me find me." (Proverbs 8:17)

Those who are truly looking to make God a significant part of their lives find him. This is why you find so many calling their association with God a relationship. Although they may only go to church once a week, the time a person devotes to knowing God and relying on him for direction and solitude is much more valuable to them than the time spent with others watching the local football team, and it means much more to God. This is why he loves those who diligently seek him, as he has sacrificed for you. He also wants you to sacrifice some of yourself for him.

So are you sacrificing yourself for God? What promises do you have that God will make your sacrifices worth enduring? What guarantees do you have that God is someone you can trust to serve and your service will even be acknowledged?

You can trust that God has recognized your sacrifice as he has acknowledged the sacrifices of those before, and the sacrifices of those before you have allowed them to achieve great things. We can see this in Galatians 3:5–9,

> So again I ask, does God give you his Spirit and work miracles among you by the works of the law, or by your believing what you heard? So also Abraham believed God, and it was credited to him as righteousness. Understand, then, that those who have faith are children of Abraham. Scripture foresaw that God would justify the Gentiles by faith, and announced the gospel in advance to Abraham: "All nations will be blessed through you." So those who rely on faith are blessed along with Abraham, the man of faith.

By having faith in God, we have the same relationship of trust that Abraham had in God, and we have miles and miles of evidence that having faith in God is beneficial to people. When Abraham placed his trust in God, he did not have an Old Testament that cited example after example of how God had provided for people who had placed their trust in him above everything else. These examples included their livelihood, other needs that had been met, or miracles performed on their behalf. Nor did Abraham have the New Testament and the words of the Son of the living God to reinforce that what was asked of God through faith would be provided. Still he trusted God and was given back more than he could have possibly imagined.

You and I are granted the same trust as Abraham through the same faith he had. It is not a different faith even though God spoke to Abraham. God has expressed to us through Christ in the New Testament many times that trusting in him is the same as having faith in God. So we can trust in God just as Abraham trusted in God and know that our faith is what God is looking for in us, and he will provide for our needs, the same as he did for Abraham.

You may say that to expect God to provide for you, the same as he did for Abraham cannot be expected as Abraham was the father of many nations, but God treasures you just as much, as is evidenced by the scriptures, "Commit your way to the LORD; trust in him and he will do this: He will make your righteous reward shine like the dawn, your vindication like the noonday sun." (Psalm 37:5–6)

As Abraham committed himself and trusted in the Lord, God saw this commitment and gave great benefits to Abraham and all of his descendants. If you pledge yourself to the Lord, trusting in him to see you through, he will act to help you, the same as Abraham. In our lives, at many times, much the same as it was for Abraham, it is hard to see that trusting in God is going to provide for our needs. But throughout scripture, we are assured that it will, and we have seen throughout, especially in the Old Testament, that God will provide for those who take actions that rely on trusting in God. Through these actions, God builds trust with each of us, according to our own needs and abilities. For if God is able to gain our trust in him, then he is able to accomplish the best for us.

This is illustrated best in Proverbs 3:5–6, "Trust in the LORD with all your heart, and lean not on your own understanding; in all your ways submit to him, and he will make your paths straight."

For us at many times, it is hard to see that God is providing the best way for us, as we are limited to what we see and oftentimes cannot perceive beyond whatever we are struggling with or refuse to try to look further than our current struggles, as situations in life oftentimes become so all-consuming that we are incapable of seeing any further than what is currently in front of us. In these times, we should trust in God, but not only place our trust in him. As the scripture in Proverbs says, we should also acknowledge God. That is, we should show God that we are trusting in him through our prayers, worship, and giving of ourselves to him.

I know this is a hard thing for most of us, to cede control of yourself to someone else, especially somebody who mostly works through people's lives through words in a book. But I am sure you will find as you study the Bible that many verses you read apply to what you are going through in life. In fact, if you just did a web search, you will find page after page of testimony by people who have had their lives changed for the better simply by reading the Bible. God is able to do this because in their lives he has seen every decision they could make and each path they could take. So when people are ready to listen to the Word of God through the Bible or begin searching it for help, the answers they were looking for were waiting for them the whole time.

This is a very difficult leap of faith to make, as most of us naturally look to ourselves or others we know that have earned our trust over time. The often-used phrase, "stick with what you know," applies here. It is so much more comfortable for us to make decisions and overcome issues in our lives with those we know and trust. It is so much harder for us to have faith in someone we cannot see or dial the phone and talk to.

But as I have shown throughout this book, the one you are trusting in now is the one who placed the earth perfectly from the sun so it could support life for billions of people. If there is anyone to trust with your life, it is God, and he assures us of this, "Have I not commanded you? Be strong and courageous. Do not be afraid; do not be discouraged, for the LORD your God will be with you wherever you go." (Joshua 1:9)

This God understands that you will be afraid at times, indecisive occasionally, and doubtful at times, but in all of these moments, he is telling you not to be because he is with you and he is there to see you through these things and any other event in your life. You can tell this is true simply by reading the words of the Bible. He shows over and over that he has plans for the best in your life.

For most of us, we feel we must make every decision because we always know what is best for us. Even if we are unsure of what the results may be, we are sure that whatever we think is best is best, and this is why God asks us to trust in him because we cannot see everything. But God can! This is why we see verses such as this in Proverbs 3:5, "Trust in the LORD with all your heart; and lean not to your own understanding."

We should trust in God for direction in life and seek his Word when we are unsure. There is example after example of people who have sought direction in their lives through the Word of God and found their lives improved by doing it. Actor Mark Wahlberg, who spent time in prison as a teenager, credits his faith as the most important element in his restoration. The late singer Donna Summers was a devout Christian, and legendary rocker Alice Cooper overcame some of his struggles by taking every word in the Bible literally. An editor of the Huffington Post, Craig Kannalley, wrote that his life was changed in a short span of time by reading the Bible daily. He stated that things started happening to him for the better, and he developed a clear mission and became happier. Many of the words in the Bible spoke directly to him.

These things happened in their lives the same as they will in your life and mine, and this is because, when we trust in God and look to him by reading his Word, he leads us to a greater and more fulfilling life. His Word was handed down not to reach just one of us or a select few, but each of us in times of need, struggles, and for reassurance or even further enrichment of joys that we are already experiencing. The power of the Word can do these things for all of us.

When Ruth followed her mother-in-law Naomi to Bethlehem, she surrendered herself to an unknown future, but she did so because she trusted two things: Naomi, with whom she had developed a loving relationship, and God. Ruth trusted Naomi because the two women had a shared history and loved the same people. They had seen good and bad times together. Ruth knew Naomi was no fool and her mother-in-law loved her.

Perhaps she felt she owed it to her dead husband to look after his mother. We are kept in the dark about the relationship between Ruth and Naomi's son. More importantly, Ruth also trusted God to protect her, but not from harm or worry because that comes to everyone. God does not shield us from these things. We do not live in a cocoon simply because we trust in God. But Ruth said, "Whatever happens, I know it is God's plan. Even if I do not understand it, I hand my future over to God."

The result? Ruth was a foreigner, a woman, a widow without children, and thus a second-class citizen in ancient Israel. Despite these handicaps, she won, and the story ends by describing her as "better than seven sons" to Naomi.

A further example of Proverbs 3:5 from the Bible is Isaac. Compared to other Bible characters, Isaac's life was quiet. His faith was real but was not full of exciting events like Noah and Abraham. Even though his life was quiet, it still contained many lessons that would be helpful to us. Just think of what it might have been like to be Abraham's son. Imagine some of the great stories about God's providing for and blessing him. Abraham probably shared some of his mistakes as well as his adventures, and Isaac must have learned much about how faith worked. He shared with him the many promises that God made and how God always kept them. It is important to remember that our faith always rests on God keeping his promises. The whole life of Abraham was about how faithful God was. We can be certain that Isaac believed that as well.

Back in those days, there were no radios, televisions, or computers to give us information, so the family gathered, talked, and shared life stories. It was the main source of education as well. Just think of what it is like to hear our parents talk about how good God is and how he always came through when they were in need. Abraham's faith influenced Isaac, as we will see as our story continues. Think about your parents telling what happened when you were little and growing up. They told you about something interesting that you did. That is what Isaac experienced as a child, hearing his father Abraham tell these wonderful true stories.

But hearing stories about someone else's faith is not the same as seeing God work in your own life. Isaac had to come to the place where he had to have his own experience of faith. As altars were a reminder of God's faithfulness to Abraham, now Isaac was going to have an altar of his own to remember.

One day Isaac went with Abraham to a top of a mountain to offer to God a sacrifice. He helped his father gather wood and build a stone altar. As he looked around, a question came into his mind, "Father, look. We have wood and an altar, but where is the animal we are to place on the altar?"

Isaac did not know that God had spoken to Abraham before and told him that he was to offer his son as a sacrifice. Abraham knew what was to happen, but Isaac didn't. Imagine his surprise when he saw his father carefully laying him on the stack of wood and tying him there. What do you think Isaac must have thought? Maybe he asked, "Father, why are you doing this to me?"

Abraham at the same time must have been asking, "Why do I have to do this?" But Abraham obeyed God once again and remembered that the heavenly Father said he would bless Abraham through his son Isaac.

How far was Abraham willing to obey God? Abraham comforted Isaac by saying, "God will provide a Lamb." Later the Bible tells us that Abraham believed, if his son died, God would raise Isaac from the dead.

Just as Abraham was about to kill Isaac, God called out and told him not to do so. And being true to his promise, he provided a ram to take Isaac's place. That was Isaac's first altar experience and one he would remember for the rest of his life! He had an experience of a ram taking his place on the altar, just like Jesus did for us when he died for our sins on the cross.

This was a test of Isaac's faith as well as Abraham's. Isaac was willing to trust God even when he didn't understand why. Sometimes we need to be like Isaac. God has given our parents to us, and occasionally they ask us to do that which seems unreasonable, but faith is believing in God when nothing makes sense. Someday it will, if we are patient and willing for God to show us why in his time.

Perhaps we can say that he learned from Abraham's mistake as well as Abraham did. He made an effort to make certain that Isaac married the right person, and we can say he stayed happily married for the rest of his life with Rebekah. Isaac was a quiet person, and he showed his faith in practical ways. He did not hastily try to find someone to marry but left the choice of his life's mate to God. Sometimes we get in a hurry and want something right away, and when we do that, we make wrong choices.

Someday you, like Isaac, may have to wait for the right time and the right person to come along. It is important to leave our need for marriage in God's hands. Isaac's wife was both beautiful and faithful. Faithfulness is a character quality that everyone should seek. For many years, Isaac and Rebekah could have no children. It was not easy for older people to be without children. If you didn't have children in those days, people thought you were strange. (As if it were your fault.)

Once again, God had promised that Isaac would have children so they waited for God to act. Isaac was forty years old when he married Rebekah, and they did not have children until twenty years later. I know of married couples who could not have children for years. They decided to adopt, and once they did, they had three more children of their own. I'm sure they learned a lesson on how God works. Isaac waited for God's time, and finally the day came when Rebekah gave birth to twin boys.

Isaac had his weaknesses. A similar experience happened to him like that of Abraham. Because there was famine in the land, Isaac headed to a place called Gerar, where there was food and water. He came before King Abimelech and told him that Rebekah was his sister. You would think that he would have learned from Abraham's mistake, but we often learn the best lessons from our own mistakes. Once again, God stepped in and kept Isaac from harm.

God blessed Isaac with great riches. Sometimes being rich isn't that great because it often has many temptations that come with it. Isaac's riches caused him to be generous and did not leave him selfish. Five times, he dug wells of water, and each time someone came and took them away from him. He never fought to get them back or blamed them for being mean. He just let them have it and moved on to dig another one. Isaac became an experienced well digger, but well digging was not the purpose God had in mind for him. Often God uses our talents to be a blessing to others. Isaac was a good example to us of what it means to be unselfish. Isaac realized that what he had was from God. He had no problem sharing them with others. When we take the attitude that God owns all we have and it is his, giving it away becomes no problem.

People took advantage of Isaac's generosity, like they do to everyone else. Even when he was old and could no longer see, his wife and son took advantage of him to get something for themselves. Isaac was big enough to accept the tricks they played and forgave them later. Isaac and Rebekah waited twenty years to have their children. Isaac learned how to wait on God, and God never failed to provide for his every need. He will do that for you as well when you place your trust in him.

And one of the most famous of those who trusted in God and was given great reward was Noah and the legendary flood. It had been many decades since God had told Noah that he would not put up with such evil forever. In fact, he had set 120 years as the limit without saying what would happen. Clearly he had something big in mind, and now whatever it would be was getting much closer.

Noah knew that God was God, so he should be served, trusted, and obeyed. Noah did exactly that. He did all his business honestly and truthfully because he knew God, and his enterprises prospered, bringing him great wealth. He was true to his wife because he knew God. And he worked to suppress evil as best he could, all because he knew God. But fewer and fewer cared. In fact, by now Noah did not know anyone outside his family who really trusted God.

Then God spoke to Noah again, and this time it really blew his mind. He told Noah to build a really massive boat, more like a multi-deck barge actually. It was to be much bigger than any boats that had ever been built. He was to do this because God said he was going to wipe out all people and land-dwelling animals by flooding the entire earth. God would send to Noah some of all the types of land animals so the new world could be repopulated after the flood.

Noah said the boat didn't need to be taken to water because the water was going to come to it. Who ever heard such a thing? The years came and went, and it was getting close to being finished. The thousands of animal stalls and cages were going in.

One day Noah announced there were seven days to go. If anyone wanted to join him and his family and miss out on the great dying, then they were quite welcome. A number of his friends were tempted but weren't really convinced, and they didn't want to be seen as fools like Noah.

Sure, he was a nice guy and a good friend. He talked too much about God, but he was honest and thoughtful, and he always helped you when you needed it. Seven days to go and not an animal in one of the cages on board that boat! He had to be nuts. Some began having second thoughts when animals started arriving. Then the countryside seemed to turn into a walking zoo. They saw animals, including many they had never seen before, and birds flew in from all directions. It was as though they all had compasses zeroed in on the boat out in the middle of Noah's property. And they kept on pouring in, day after day. It would have been incredibly unnerving to witness something so unique as just a couple of each type of animal showing up at the same spot, the ark that Noah was building. There were no herds of animals.

I'm sure without much speculation on your own part that you can imagine a carnival atmosphere had developed, with fast-food stalls and buskers on the main road feeding and entertaining the thousands of onlookers. And now the day had arrived, and the roads were packed with people who had come to have a real laugh at old Noah. But if the past week had been unnerving with all the animals arriving, it would have been positively weird that all of a sudden the regular stream of animals stopped. Talk about eerie, but most likely, the people kept giving Noah a hard time even with all of the strange happenings from the animals. And when it died down, you can imagine Noah gave them one last chance with a speech that probably went a little something like this,

> I want to thank those who helped me so much in working on this project. I am deeply grateful. I've talked to many of you over these past years about why this boat has been built. I've told you that God is

patient and kind and does not want anyone to perish, but his patience was running out. I have urged you to turn from your rebellion against God and your selfish ways and to trust God and join me when the day arrives. Relatives, friends, and neighbors, *the day has arrived!* You can come and join my family and me now if you believe what God has said. If not, I'm sorry, but I have to say good-bye. You will never see me again.

Then the next day, what was that? Did the ground move? There it was again. The ground shook and swayed, throwing everyone off their feet. Huge cracks snaked across the countryside. Water began shooting out of the ground like massive fountains, and fire and steam could be seen pouring out of the distant hills. The sky was now black. Incredibly violent rain began, and in the deepening, surging waters, Noah's boat began to float.

After nearly six weeks, the endless din of pounding rain stopped. Their five-month ride on a world without land had finally come to an end. For seven more months, they waited, in which time the land began to appear from beneath the water, and the shaking gradually diminished. The world-destroying cataclysm, God's judgment on a wicked world, was over. Three hundred and seventy-one days later, over a year after the door was shut, they opened it and came out along with the animals. They were in a new world.

Noah trusted what God said about the flood, even when no one had ever seen such a thing. Because he trusted God, Noah built the ark. And in doing so, he and his family became the only ones who were not destroyed. And because he trusted God, all of us are here. All of us, even the world's skeptics, are descendants of the families of Noah's three sons, Shem, Ham, and Japheth.

Joseph in the Bible is one of the greatest heroes of the Old Testament, second perhaps only to Moses. What separated him from others was his absolute trust in God, regardless of what happened to him. He is a shining example of what can happen when a person surrenders to God and obeys completely.

In his youth, Joseph was proud, enjoying his status as his father's favorite. Joseph bragged, giving no thought to how it hurt his brothers. They became so angry with his arrogance that they threw him down a dry well and then sold him into slavery to a passing caravan.

Taken to Egypt, Joseph was sold again to Potiphar, an official in Pharaoh's household. Through hard work and humility, Joseph rose to the position of overseer of Potiphar's entire estate. But Potiphar's wife lusted after Joseph. When Joseph rejected her sinful advance, she lied and said Joseph tried to rape her. Potiphar had Joseph thrown into prison.

Joseph must have wondered why he was being punished for doing the right thing, just the same as you or I do when we are doing what is right and the best we can do and still nothing goes right for us. Even though nothing seemed to be going right for Joseph, he kept trusting in God to see him through his circumstances and continued to work hard, and he was eventually put in charge of all the prisoners. As two of the Pharaoh's servants were hauled into prison, each told Joseph about his dreams.

Now God had given Joseph the gift of interpreting dreams. He told the cupbearer his dream meant he would be freed and returned to his former position. Joseph also told the baker his dream meant he would be hanged, and both interpretations proved true.

Two years later, Pharaoh had a dream, and the cupbearer remembered Joseph's gift. Joseph interpreted Pharaoh's dream, and his God-given wisdom was so great that Pharaoh put Joseph in charge of all of Egypt. And while in a position of authority, Joseph stockpiled grain to avoid a terrible famine.

Later Joseph's brothers came to Egypt to buy food, and after many tests, Joseph revealed himself to them. He forgave them and then sent for their father, Jacob, and the rest of his people. They all came to Egypt and settled in land that Pharaoh gave them. Out of much adversity, Joseph saved the twelve tribes of Israel, God's chosen people.

Joseph trusted God no matter how bad his situation got and eventually was put in a position to save not only his own people but all of Egypt from starvation. Just like with Joseph, God will give us strength to endure our painful circumstances. We have to trust in him that he will see us through. "Those who know your name will trust in you, for you, LORD, have never forsaken those who seek you." (Psalm 9:10)

This is why you can trust that, by reading the Word of God, you will find verses that can help you with issues you are struggling with, what you are going through in life at the current time, or ways to just improve upon your life. When you are seeking God through his Word, you are allowing God to help you and since our heavenly Father is omnipotent, most likely the words that you read from scripture will be verses that provide the help or healing you are seeking at that time. You see, God knows what you need to hear or read all along your journey in life as he gave you life. He also gives you support and comfort in his Word throughout your life.

You can rely on God as shown from the examples of those in the Bible who have trusted him and prospered. Abraham did not know where God was leading him, but he trusted God in faith. Even though Abraham was led for many years on a journey that showed little promise, he remained faithful. At many times, he lived like a nomad with nothing more over his head than a tent. But God delivered to Abraham a great nation of people, as he promised he would, and he will do the same for you and me. It may not be in the timeline that you want him to deliver on promises, but you have to realize that your timeline is limited and God's is unlimited. He can see past your timeline and knows when you need him most to step in and support you.

We can see this in David as well. David had to wander throughout the land and sleep in caves as Saul tried to kill him many times to keep David from replacing Saul as king, but God protected David and kept him on a path that would avoid Saul until David could become king. David learned that, even though he may fail God, he could trust in his heavenly Father to be faithful to David as can be seen in Psalm 106:1, "Praise the LORD. Give thanks to the LORD, for he is good; his love endures forever."

You and I are seeking trust in the same God that Abraham, Isaac, David, Ruth, Noah, and Joseph trusted. And as with them, our trust in God has to partner with our faith in God that he will see us through times, circumstances, and periods in our lives that seem to test our trust because we are not omnipotent like God. This is why we also must trust God over man because "It is better to take refuge in the LORD than to trust in humans." (Psalm 118:8)

As I am sure we all have lost count of how many times our fellow man has failed us or come up short of our expectations, that is to be expected as man is selfish and self-oriented. He can justify immoral decisions and is limited in his abilities. However, God is none of these. Because he is unlimited and omnipotent, he is there to help us and meet our needs when we are needing him most. All of the examples I have laid out in this chapter have proven this over and over. The best decision for us is to place our trust in God. And the best reason to do that is because of the love God has for us. As the apostle Paul said,

> Love is patient, love is kind. It does not envy, it does not boast, it is not proud. It does not dishonor others, it is not self-seeking, it is not easily angered, it keeps no record of wrongs. Love does not delight in evil but rejoices with the truth. It always protects, always trusts, always hopes, always perseveres. (1 Corinthians 13:4–7)

chapter 5
Bigness of God

Now that you have seen in the previous chapter why you should trust God with your life as the people of the Bible trusted God with their lives. He always kept his promises, and he always did what was best for the people of the Bible according to his plans for their lives. You might want to know how you can trust God.

A good place to start when trying to gain an understanding of just how big God is—for example, how he is able to be working in your life and be there when you need him when there are billions of other people on the earth and hundreds of billions of other animals that may be in some need of him at the same time—is to start in Isaiah 40. There is so much in Isaiah 40 to show just how vast God is that the mere acknowledgement of his abilities in comparison to our own should make us question why any of us would want to reject God's help and guidance.

> Who has measured the waters in the hollow of his hand, or with the breadth of his hand marked off the heavens? Who has held the dust of the earth in a basket, or weighed the mountains on the scales and the hills in a balance? Who can fathom the Spirit of the LORD, or instruct the LORD as his counselor? Whom did the LORD consult to enlighten him, and who taught him

the right way? Who was it that taught him knowledge, or showed him the path of understanding? Surely the nations are like a drop in a bucket; they are regarded as dust on the scales; he weighs the islands as though they were fine dust. (Isaiah 40:12–15)

As you can see from Isaiah 40, man just has no idea of the capabilities of God. Our entire lives depend on the safety and stability that the earth provides, and it amounts to nothing God needs more than a basket to take care of. Isaiah is right then to ask, "Who can 'instruct the Lord as his counselor?'" Exactly no person could. No one would have any idea on how to place planets in perfect orbits that could sustain life or where to place our asteroid belt so the earth wasn't under constant threat of the millions of objects in the belt hitting its towns and cities.

No one could teach God the right way to create birds so they could fly. I mean, man learned to build planes by watching and studying birds. If there were no birds, only clouds and wind, there would be nothing as evidence that flight was achievable with the possible exception of leaves falling to the ground or animals such as the flying squirrel. Without God having first created birds, it is likely then man wouldn't have flown even today, considering the Wright brothers first flew just over a hundred years ago.

God enabled the world to serve man and his interests. But let's not limit God to just this world. To gain a better perspective on just how great he is, let's look at Psalm 147:4–5, "He determines the number of the stars and calls them each by name. Great is our Lord and mighty in power; his understanding has no limit."

And we can refer again along the same lines of Psalms with Isaiah 40:25–26,

"To whom will you compare me? Or who is my equal?" says the Holy One. Lift up your eyes and look to the heavens: Who created all these? He who brings out the starry host one by one and calls forth each of them by name. Because of his great power and mighty strength, not one of them is missing.

Now the estimate of stars in the universe is 300 sextillion. That is 3 trillion times 100 billion, and God has placed all of them. Let's just imagine what a feat that is. He has placed an infinite number of stars in the universe, and when you're considering many trillion of anything, I think it is safe to say that the term "infinite" can be used.

In addition to that infinite number of stars, there are most likely anywhere from one to hundreds of planets orbiting each of them when you consider our sun is not a particularly big star. It is likely that the larger stars could sustain many more orbits than those that our sun supports. So we are now talking about multiple trillions of objects placed in the universe, and yet the universe and particularly our solar system remains mostly at peace and in order. When he knows where to place 300 sextillion stars in the universe, he can surely know when you are going to need him most in your life.

Astronomers are not reporting regularly that planets and stars are colliding into each other, and there are no yearly reports of asteroids hitting any of the planets in our solar system despite the asteroid belt with millions of objects that could easily be set on a collision course with any planet simply by bumping into each other in the orbit they travel.

No, we live on Earth, where everything as far as living on this planet goes relatively well. Our nearest neighbors, Mars and Venus, can't support life and would kill off any life as we know it if it tried to exist there without living within a life-sustaining vessel of some sort that would have to be regularly resupplied from Earth. The Earth also faces weekly solar flares from the sun. These solar flares can reach up to one-sixth of the energy output from the sun, and they travel all the way to Earth, a distance of over 93 million miles. Yet they do not impact the Earth's atmosphere enough to threaten the daily life of anything on it.

Just think that through. The sun sends these solar flares out weekly, and they are so large that they pass through the orbits of Mercury and Venus like they are standing still and make it to the Earth's atmosphere. Yet because of how the Earth's atmosphere is composed, our planet and all of us living on it face no greater threat than having trouble getting a good signal on our cell phones. And the Earth is placed 93 million miles from the sun.

I'm not sure what the number is, but if the Earth were a million miles or maybe it's just ten thousand miles closer to the sun, one strong solar flare could be so devastating that entire regions of the world might have to go underground anytime one was going to hit them head-on. But God knew the distance to place the Earth so we would be okay. The same God who knew where to place the Earth before it was formed is the one who knew you before you were formed in the womb. If God is powerful enough to place the Earth and stars so they live in peace, then it is almost foolish for us not to seek him to give us greater peace.

Of course, it is difficult for most of us to relate to a solar flare, millions of asteroids, or 93 million miles, as our reference point is living on Earth. Even astronomers or astronauts probably have a hard time equating just how limitless God is in relation to us as they may observe the asteroid belt or witness the effects of a solar flare on a region of Earth. But they are not experiencing these things, and that is usually when people can best grasp just how big God is. Through our own life experiences, the awesomeness of God is revealed to us.

So let's take something that most of us have experienced to grant us a good idea of how big God is and how small we are by comparison, and even though we amount to less than a pinprick on the face of the Earth, God is there with us. And that experience is being out on the ocean.

Some went out on the sea in ships; they were merchants on the mighty waters. They saw the works of the LORD, his wonderful deeds in the deep. For he spoke and stirred up a tempest that lifted high the waves. They mounted up to the heavens and went down to the depths; in their peril their courage melted away. They reeled and staggered like drunkards; they were at their wits' end. Then they cried out to the LORD in their trouble, and he brought them out of their distress. He stilled the storm to a whisper; the waves of the sea were hushed. They were glad when it grew calm, and he guided them to their desired haven. (Psalm 107:23–30)

As you can see, despite thousands of years of improvement in ship building and the ability to forecast weather and ocean patterns, the sea has still remained something that man has no control over and is at the mercy of at all times. In the time of King David, mariners were looked at with some reverence for crossing the Mediterranean, something that most today would not consider a great feat. It was an event considered to be very dangerous, and not surviving it was common.

But even today, stories of people lost at sea or a boat capsizing is a common occurrence. By comparison, a plane crash of any size is uncommon and usually subject to a complete investigation. But to this day, man has no mastery of the sea and can be completely helpless at a moment's notice with no one to call on for help except God.

You can most likely relate to this, as so many of us have been out on the ocean. You may have gotten caught in the undertow and pulled out to sea far enough that you experienced some worry that you might need help to get back to land, have been stung or bitten by one of the millions of sea creatures, or just laid out in the water and come to the realization of how immense and powerful the ocean is in comparison to the small dot you are placing upon it.

If you can think back to an experience such as one of those, you can gain a sense of how immense God is and how he can oversee everything that goes on in the world's oceans and still know when he is going to need to be there to move the currents you are swimming in or against to lead you closer to him.

When trying to conceptualize the enormity of God, I think many of us would relate to David in Psalm 8:3–4, "When I consider your heavens, the work of your fingers, the moon and the stars, which you have set in place, what is mankind that you are mindful of them, human beings that you care for them?"

David, just like many of us, wondered when considering just how much God has done and continues to do throughout the entire universe. Why he would be concerned at all with our well-being?

Now you may not know, but the David in this verse of Psalms was a shepherd, so he most likely had a lot of time to think about God and reflect on the universe while he looked into the night sky as he watched over his flock. And he could think about how he fit into everything and why God would care about some lowly shepherd.

Now most of us have cell phones, televisions, and the latest celebrity gossip to keep us from often getting into much deep thought, but just like David did, we occasionally realize the immense power of God and wonder how he will fit each of us and the many twists and turns our lives will take into everything that God has done and will do.

However, the truth is that God can be there for us at every turn we may take, precisely because he is the same heavenly Father who placed trillions of stars and multiple trillions of planets all over the universe and maintains order over all of them. Because God has the authority to set the universe in motion and keep it in peace and order, he can do the same for your life if you will seek him out through scripture and prayer.

All right, so by now you may be agreeing that our God is a God of unlimited power and authority in that he can create and rule an entire universe orderly. But that doesn't mean that he knows what is best for me at all times. What you are failing to realize here is that our God is also a God of unlimited wisdom. Refer back to the quote from Isaiah 40 at the beginning of this chapter, "Who has understood the Spirit of the LORD or instructed him as his counselor?"

The answer to that question is: no one has because there has never been anything that God has not already known the answer to. So if the depths of God's wisdom have no bounds (and they do not), then we would be fools not to seek what his plans are for our lives, and sticking to our own thoughts and plans is most likely going to lead to some mistakes and failures along the way. To question someone's plans for your life who placed the Earth in the perfect orbit from the sun to sustain life may just be the very definition of foolishness.

Just think about the many twists and turns that your life has taken so far. I imagine, if you think back through either your work or your personal life, you can come up with more incidents than you can count in which you just missed a devastating blow to your career, or you may have kept yourself from doing something in a personal relationship that could have affected you for years to come, if not your whole life.

Well, how many instances do you think that God intervened for you to avoid terrible consequences or to provide a better path for you? It is likely that this has happened to many of us. At times, things turned out better than we ever could've imagined, or we just seemed to make a deadline or some commitment that we did not think we would but were already obligated to. Some people call this luck, but persons of faith should really consider that this is the greatness of God's prevenience acting in your life, the same way it acted to place the Earth perfectly from the sun to sustain our lives.

However, this is why the everlasting and all-knowing God should be sought out as the guide for all of your life, as he knows your life better than you ever will. Paul relates this idea in Galatians 4:9a, "But now that you know God—or rather are known by God."

This God is the God that created the universe, so he knew you before your birth. And if he knew you before you were born, then he also knows where you are going to need him in your life, no matter what choices you make or how many times you change the direction you are planning on living. Wow! How big is our God?

chapter 6
Jesus Is God Friending Us

So now you know that you have this immense God who is all-knowing and all-seeing who could hold all the water in the world's oceans in his hands and has created galaxies upon galaxies of stars and planets. How is this God even capable of relating to my needs of stretching a paycheck to feed the kids and pay for new brakes this month, or why is he going to be someone to lean on as you keep taking verbal abuse from your husband who seemed to change overnight?

God knew you would have problems like these all along and being able to communicate with a God that is so far removed from the problems we all face in our daily lives would not be possible. The distance between man's abilities and God's is so great that our heavenly Father had no other choice but to become one of us in order to bring about the very personal relationship that can occur between people and allow for the same type of relationship with God himself. This is exactly what God accomplished through Jesus Christ. And this was part of the plan all along, to get us to look to God for help as we look to Christ for the ultimate help of our salvation.

I know, to much of the world, even the mention of the name Jesus can be divisive to some and off-putting to many, which is quite ironic as the easiest relationship to have and the simplest to start is a relationship with God through Jesus Christ. We may have an area or areas of life that need our attention or are giving us difficulties, and it may seem like we have to take care of it all ourselves or that no one is willing to help. Well, God cuts through all of those things and makes a beeline to be there for you through a relationship with Jesus Christ. If that is not the ultimate example that God has you in mind first, last, and always even with every responsibility he has, I do not know what is.

The gift of grace through Jesus Christ is the ultimate circle to bring us back to God, and the simplicity of it stops so many of us. Many of us think that, once we accept grace through Jesus, we are duty-bound for the rest of our lives to a straight and narrow path, and coming up short or venturing away from the path once we have gotten on it is a total failure and slap in the face to God. However, let me restate who we are having a relationship with when we begin one with Jesus Christ.

When we start having a relationship with God through Jesus Christ, we are starting one with someone who knows all of our days and every choice we have made. I think we can see this best from the story of Jesus and the woman at the well as told in John 4:1–26,

> Now Jesus learned that the Pharisees had heard that he was gaining and baptizing more disciples than John although in fact it was not Jesus who baptized, but his disciples. So he left Judea and went back once more to Galilee. Now he had to go through Samaria. So he came to a town in Samaria called Sychar, near the plot of ground Jacob had given to his son Joseph. Jacob's well was there, and Jesus, tired as he was from the journey, sat down by the well. It was about noon. When a Samaritan woman came to draw water, Jesus said to her, "Will you give me a drink?"
>
> The Samaritan woman said to him, "You are a

CIRCLE TO GOD

Jew and I am a Samaritan woman. How can you ask me for a drink?"

Jesus answered her, "If you knew the gift of God and who it is that asks you for a drink, you would have asked him and he would have given you living water."

"Sir," the woman said, "you have nothing to draw with and the well is deep. Where can you get this living water? Are you greater than our father Jacob, who gave us the well and drank from it himself, as did also his sons and his livestock?"

Jesus answered, "Everyone who drinks this water will be thirsty again, but whoever drinks the water I give them will never thirst. Indeed, the water I give them will become in them a spring of water welling up to eternal life."

The woman said to him, "Sir, give me this water so that I won't get thirsty and have to keep coming here to draw water."

He told her, "Go, call your husband and come back."

"I have no husband," she replied.

Jesus said to her, "You are right when you say you have no husband. The fact is, you have had five husbands, and the man you now have is not your husband. What you have just said is quite true."

"Sir," the woman said, "I can see that you are a prophet. Our ancestors worshiped on this mountain, but you Jews claim that the place where we must worship is in Jerusalem."

"Woman," Jesus replied, "believe me, a time is coming when you will worship the Father neither on this mountain nor in Jerusalem. You Samaritans worship

- 57 -

what you do not know; we worship what we do know, for salvation is from the Jews. Yet a time is coming and has now come when the true worshipers will worship the Father in the Spirit and in truth, for they are the kind of worshipers the Father seeks. God is spirit, and his worshipers must worship in the Spirit and in truth."

The woman said, "I know that Messiah" [called Christ] "is coming. When he comes, he will explain everything to us."

Then Jesus declared, "I, the one speaking to you—I am he."

The same as with the Samaritan woman, God knows your days and needs and can bring you to a better life just by having a relationship with him. This is part of his plan for bringing Jesus into the world. He knew that you, I, and the Samaritan woman would have struggles in this life and a distant God would be difficult to lean on when you have need, but if this God lived a human life and encountered many of the same experiences that you do in life, then calling upon him and seeking his counsel is an easy thing to do.

We can see that God had this in mind all along in the scriptures. In Isaiah 43:19, we can see that God had already been working for the betterment of people he favored, "See, I am doing a new thing! Now it springs up; do you not perceive it? I am making a way in the wilderness and streams in the wasteland."

You can see, even though this time in the lives of the Israelites is bad, God is setting up a greater future than they could have ever imagined. The Israelites cannot see it as they, like you and I, are generally concerned with their daily lives and do not have the limitless vision that God has to see that he is making things better for them, but as it is written in Hebrews 10:1, "The law is only a shadow of the good things that are coming—not the realities themselves."

The old covenant God made with the Israelites was nothing from which they would have perceived the new covenant that God would bring to the world through Jesus Christ. What has happened with Christ is that essentially the top-down relationship of God to man has been completely redone. We are now brought into a relationship to God, with the following understanding,

> For he chose us in him before the creation of the world to be holy and blameless in his sight. In love he predestined us for adoption to sonship through Jesus Christ, in accordance with his pleasure and will-to the praise of his glorious grace, which he has freely given us in the One he loves. (Ephesians 1:4–6)

Similar to a marriage, we are now united with Christ. But unlike a marriage, God chose to join us with him long before the foundation of the world. This is a point missed by so many people who turn off completely anytime the name of Jesus is even mentioned. God knew ahead of time that all of us would come up short of his standards, as his standards are perfection. He knew that we would do or desire things that were not best for us or would create wedges between ourselves and God. And despite all of those things, he wanted us to be with him and a part of him. We can see Jesus confirm that he is the way to God through his own words,

> "I have testimony weightier than that of John. For the works that the Father has given me to finish—the very works that I am doing—testify that the Father has sent me. And the Father who sent me has himself testified concerning me. You have never heard his voice nor seen his form, nor does his word dwell in you, for you do not believe the one he sent. You study the

scriptures diligently because you think that in them you have eternal life. These are the very scriptures that testify about me, yet you refuse to come to me to have life."

"I do not accept glory from human beings, but I know you. I know that you do not have the love of God in your hearts. I have come in my Father's name, and you do not accept me; but if someone else comes in his own name, you will accept him. How can you believe since you accept glory from one another but do not seek the glory that comes from the only God?"

"But do not think I will accuse you before the Father. Your accuser is Moses, on whom your hopes are set. If you believed Moses, you would believe me, for he wrote about me. But since you do not believe what he wrote, how are you going to believe what I say?" (John 5:36–47)

As you can see, Jesus is saying that the people are coming to God under the old covenant, but even Moses himself was pointing to Jesus, and God was testifying to Jesus's coming. It was important for scriptures to lead up to Jesus, as he is the key to every one of us knowing and having an everlasting relationship with God.

As I have mentioned throughout this book, we live under the God who created the entire universe. There was just no way we could relate to him. In order for God to be a part of our lives, he had to live among us. He had to live through all of the daily trials and tribulations that we do to know when we would need him.

This is where the magic happens, and it is all because of Christ. Many people try through many different efforts to gain a greater understanding of God, and we do not have to. This is exactly what God has done for us in Jesus Christ. God has used Christ to reveal himself to us, as we can see in John 17:25–26, "Righteous Father, though the world does not know you, I know you, and they know that you have sent me. I have made you known to them, and will continue to make you known in order that the love you have for me may be in them and that I myself may be in them."

Jesus is the one who reveals God to us. If we want to know what God is like, all we have to do is look at Jesus. If we want to know how God cares for people, we can look at how Jesus ministered to them. If we want to know God's will for our lives, we can listen to Jesus's words and know they reveal God's truth. Jesus reveals the nature of God in his actions and words. And Jesus continues to reveal God to us. He is the one through whom the fullest revelation of God comes.

Jesus is the one to focus on if we really want to know God. And how did he come to us? Not as the all-powerful God who can flood the earth and hold all of its waters in his hands. No, the immensity of God that I have talked about previously is not evident in the birth of Christ, as that would not build the bridge so each of us could establish a personal relationship with Christ, who is God incarnate.

Our God comes to us as a harmless baby in a barn, amongst farm animals, in some town that probably wouldn't even get approved to be part of the route for a highway today. He was presented as so non-threatening that even Herod himself did not take him seriously as he sent no soldiers along with the Magi to search for him,

> After Jesus was born in Bethlehem in Judea, during the time of King Herod, Magi from the east came to Jerusalem and asked, "Where is the one who has been born king of the Jews? We saw his star when it rose and have come to worship him." When King Herod heard this he was disturbed, and all Jerusalem with him. When he had called together all the people's chief priests and teachers of the law, he asked them where

the Messiah was to be born. "In Bethlehem in Judea," they replied, "for this is what the prophet has written: 'But you, Bethlehem, in the land of Judah, are by no means least among the rulers of Judah; for out of you will come a ruler who will shepherd my people Israel.'" (Matthew 2:1–6)

I mean it was prophesized that a ruler was going to command all of the Israelites! You would think, if the word had gotten out that this person had come into adulthood, the nearby king, in this case, Herod, would send out some soldiers to take care of the threat. But a baby! You are not very worried and consider you have plenty of time to squash that threat.

It is quite fitting that Jesus is referred to as the Lamb as he came into the world, just as defenseless as one, just like you and I did. And his time was before hospitals, vaccines, and incubators. An infant not making it past their first year was more than likely a common occurrence during his time. God knew that by having Jesus face all the threats that living life gives all of us, we would be able to see just how well God knows what we are going through.

This is why Christ is so important to all of us. Who God is and how he feels about all of us is shown through Jesus. Jesus never condemned the people struggling, the sick ones, or those who had made mistakes in their lives. Only the pious were given stern warnings. Through Christ, we can see the ultimate act of love, despite each of us coming up short at all points in our lives of the perfection that God seeks. We are all granted redemption through Christ, "Who then can be saved?" Jesus looked at them and said, "With man this is impossible, but with God all things are possible." (Matthew 19:25–26)

You can see just what God is capable of and what the redemption is that God gave us through Jesus Christ in the story of Lazarus. Lazarus's sisters, Martha and Mary, sent word to Jesus that "the man you love is ill" with the implied request that Jesus should come and heal him. But Jesus's reaction is curious. He doesn't rush off immediately to try to heal his close friend. Instead he remains where he is for two days longer while his friend dies. Then after Lazarus has died, he sets off to visit him. Jesus didn't come to rescue Lazarus, but to redeem him.

In the same manner, God did not rescue Jesus on the cross. He let him die a painful, agonizing death. However, after his death, God redeemed Jesus. And as God reveals his power of redemption through Jesus, Jesus shows us the redemption that God has granted to us through Jesus.

When thinking about what each of us goes through when considering what the Bible says Jesus is and what Jesus himself said he is, I like to think about the lives of the apostles and the way in which they accepted Jesus. There was no doubt in each of the apostles' minds that, when Jesus called "follow me" to them, they went with him, but most likely they had doubts when doing it also. Some of the apostles had yet to see Jesus perform any miracles and mainly decided to follow him just because of his words. They obeyed and did what Jesus asked. They followed him.

This, to me, is astounding! Did they just leave their families? The Bible does not say, but wherever Jesus took them, they went. Remember Jesus had no home to go to. I do not know what happened to the home of Mary and Joseph, whether they still owned or rented the home they had when Jesus lived with them. But now, at this time, Jesus was alone and slept outdoors or with someone who invited him to their home. Jesus now must be at least thirty years old.

There is no record of what conversations they had with him, whether they told him of their family or whether each went to his own home at night. They also did not stay in one place. Jesus walked, and the apostles walked with him. The apostles were likely no different than you or I today. They would want to know where they were going, how long it was going to take, or when they would next have the chance to eat something.

I mean, these were routine complaints to Moses as he led his people to the Promised Land. Did the people in Jesus's time become much more complacent from living under brutal Roman rulers? Likely no. It is more likely that they had complaints and wanted to know why they had to go to this place today, even after seeing Jesus perform some wondrous miracles.

A great example of this was when Jesus was in the garden of Gethsemane the night before his crucifixion. The Bible tells us the apostles were with him. However, they fell asleep. The Bible tells us that he wanted them to pray with him. Jesus longed for their company, especially at this time. Even if he did not know exactly what was ahead for him, he knew the storm clouds from the Romans and Pharisees were gaining strength and his future was likely to be getting much worse before it would get better, if it even did.

There were times when Jesus must not have been with them because we are told in the Bible that the men went fishing. Jesus surprised them one morning after they had been fishing the whole night, and they complained they could not catch even one fish. Peter expressed to Jesus the disappointment they had in not catching any fish. His announcement did not dismay Jesus. He told them to fish on the other side. At first, Peter did not believe it would help to change the side on which they were fishing, and he was certain that would not provide better luck. But finally the men did as Jesus told them. What happened? They caught so many fish that they had trouble with the nets and getting the fish into the boat.

It may have been the same morning Jesus was on the shore cooking breakfast for them. What a surprise! Here was Jesus waiting upon them, fixing them breakfast. It must have seemed to them that they should be serving Jesus. He was greater than they were. At least they must have felt that way since they were following and obeying him. It seems to me they were very confused.

I mean, if your boss had a meal ready to eat when you showed up to work for him, you'd think it a little odd. And the apostles were calling Jesus "Lord" at this point. It would be confusing to us, just as it probably was for the apostles regarding who Jesus really was. They were unsure of what was going on, but I believe they wanted to know more about him. And so they followed.

Somehow they must have had a life with others because we learned that Jesus was at a wedding party for a relative of theirs. What happened there must have impressed them beyond belief. There came a lull in the party when the hostess realized she had no wine left to serve. She told Jesus. What did Jesus do? He just went right ahead and changed the water to the finest wine the guests had ever tasted.

One day following a long walk, Jesus suggested they go over to the other side of the lake. The rest of the crowd also went along. There were so many people who followed him that Jesus could not make himself heard by everyone, so he talked from a boat to the people who sat in a crowd on the shore. Imagine that. Hundreds of people were wanting to know more about him, so they followed wherever he went.

The crowds were there when Jesus healed the leper. They were there when a woman was accused of adultery and saw Jesus write something on the ground. What occurred after they saw him write in the sand? All the accusers backed away and left the woman alone. Did Jesus's action have an effect then upon his disciples? Surely, the effect on the crowd was very significant. When the accusers saw the writing, they all turned and started to leave.

Then the crowd saw him at the temple. They watched the people as they paid the priests who were selling cattle and items for a sacrifice. They certainly must have been startled when they saw Jesus take out a whip and flog the money changers. He accused them of making the temple into a house of a den of thieves. They must have wondered, "What kind of man is he?" Jesus claimed his Father did not want them to make his house a house of merchandise. Who was his Father?

Jesus and the disciples saw Zaccheus, a rich, prominent publican, after passing through Jordan. They saw Zaccheus try to make his way through the crowd to find Jesus. Because he was a short and small man, he even tried climbing a tree so he could see Jesus as he passed by. What did Jesus do when he saw Zaccheus in the tree? He said, "Come down. I am going to go to your house today." This too the disciples saw. Did this not have an effect upon them? The crowd that followed must also have been confused.

Jesus turned everything upside down. In Samaria, where the Jews would not venture, was a well to which Jesus went. He sat down and watched as a woman came to the well to draw water. Jesus spoke to her, "Give me a drink of water." She looked up at him in surprise. In the first instance, men did not address women they did not know. She was surprised to hear him. Then he told her, if she would drink of the water he could give her, she would have eternal life. He also told her that her answer to him about not having a husband was true since the man she was living with was not her husband. She immediately understood he was the Messiah. She went to the village to call the men to come and see Jesus. Isn't that interesting?

When the disciples returned to the well, they must have been surprised to have learned about the discussion between him and the woman. Jesus had been talking with a woman. They then must have realized a woman could bring men to the Savior. This incident must have had a profound effect upon their understanding. It must have changed their thinking about women.

Everything Jesus did had an impact upon the disciples' lives. They must have been intrigued by him to the extent of being unable to understand, to be weakened in spirit, to change their way of thinking, and to stumble on their words, as they watched and heard what developed as they went along with him. I think we can still see examples of this happening with people all over the world today and even with you and me.

Reading the actual words of Jesus from the Bible can cause us to stumble between directions we want to go in life and where the very words of Jesus point you to go. And in other circumstances, our way of thinking and our actions can be changed, and even our entire lives can be altered because of Jesus's words. And in some cases, people's lives have been transformed by an experience they have had with Jesus.

In many cases, the changes do not take hold immediately, and sometimes changes even take years, as we do not have the advantage the apostles had of having Jesus most likely within earshot most days. But the fact that lives are still being transformed two thousand years later is a testament to how powerful Jesus's words are and how powerful an experience with Christ can be.

Jesus did other things that caused people to question if he were who he said he was. In John 6, Jesus talked about his being the bread of life. Beginning in verse 53, Jesus said to the apostles, as well as the many disciples in the crowd that followed him, unless they eat flesh of the son of man and drink his blood, they have no life in themselves.

Many of the disciples, when they heard what Jesus said, complained it was too hard to understand. Jesus asked if they were offended by what he told them. He endeavored to explain to them what he meant, but they could not believe, and many went away and no longer walked with him.

However, Jesus asked the twelve apostles if they would also go away, but they told him that he had the words of eternal life and they believed he was the Christ, the Son of the living God. Jesus reminded them he had chosen them, but one of them would betray him. I believe this was an incredibly difficult time for the apostles, and they must have had difficulty overcoming their doubts, but their belief in him remained, and they stayed with him.

Following this episode, Jesus walked in Galilee. He would not walk with the Jews. He knew the Jews sought to kill him. This was the time of the Feast of Tabernacles in Judea, and Jesus stayed in Galilee until his apostles went to the feast. Then Jesus went openly into Judea, and the Jews sought him and asked, "Where is he?" There was much murmuring about what kind of person he was. He also went up and taught in the temple, but they marveled at this because he had never been educated.

There was much murmuring and talking about who Jesus was and posturing of the Pharisees about meeting Jesus to destroy him. Think of how the apostles felt. They believed Jesus was the Messiah, but they could do nothing to change the crowd. Some believed in him; others hated him and wanted him killed.

It must have been very difficult for the apostles. They could not help him even if they had wanted to. They must have been terribly worried and confused. His life was not in their hands, but in his Father's hands.

Jesus taught them many lessons that changed the way they thought and acted. I imagine Jesus startled them many times and changed their way of behaving with women and children. They must have realized Jesus was changing everyone, even the men. Everything Jesus did was in love and fulfillment of the law, even his crucifixion.

Jesus changed the life of the apostles in every way. They were filled with the Holy Spirit and learned to become like Jesus, to love and to obey the laws of God. We too learn to obey the laws of God, to be filled with the Holy Spirit, and to believe in God's Son, Jesus.

The best example in the scriptures of how God is waiting on us to seek his redemption and to take part in the life that he has planned for us with him as a guide is the story of the road to Emmaus.

Now that same day two of them were going to a village
called Emmaus, about seven miles from Jerusalem.

They were talking with each other about everything that had happened. As they talked and discussed these things with each other, Jesus himself came up and walked along with them; but they were kept from recognizing him.

He asked them, "What are you discussing together as you walk along?"

They stood still, their faces downcast. One of them, named Cleopas, asked him, "Are you the only one visiting Jerusalem who does not know the things that have happened there in these days?"

"What things?" he asked.

"About Jesus of Nazareth," they replied. "He was a prophet, powerful in word and deed before God and all the people. The chief priests and our rulers handed him over to be sentenced to death, and they crucified him; but we had hoped that he was the one who was going to redeem Israel. And what is more, it is the third day since all this took place. In addition, some of our women amazed us. They went to the tomb early this morning but didn't find his body. They came and told us that they had seen a vision of angels, who said he was alive. Then some of our companions went to the tomb and found it just as the women had said, but they did not see Jesus."

He said to them, "How foolish you are, and how slow to believe all that the prophets have spoken! Did not the Messiah have to suffer these things and then enter his glory?" And beginning with Moses and all the Prophets, he explained to them what was said in all the scriptures concerning himself.

As they approached the village to which they were

going, Jesus continued on as if he were going farther. But they urged him strongly, "Stay with us, for it is nearly evening; the day is almost over." So he went in to stay with them.

When he was at the table with them, he took bread, gave thanks, broke it and began to give it to them. Then their eyes were opened and they recognized him, and he disappeared from their sight. They asked each other, "Were not our hearts burning within us while he talked with us on the road and opened the Scriptures to us?"

They got up and returned at once to Jerusalem. There they found the Eleven and those with them, assembled together and saying, "It is true! The Lord has risen and has appeared to Simon." Then the two told what had happened on the way, and how Jesus was recognized by them when he broke the bread. (Luke 24:13–35)

The Emmaus story is a clear reminder of how we remain oblivious to God's presence even when he's right beside us. The Emmaus disciples were blinded by their mistaken expectations about what God was doing in Jesus. Just the same as the two disciples dismissed Jesus as anything more than but a liberating figure, just three days after his death and with Jesus walking beside them, the relentless and powerful lies of today's culture also blind us to God's presence. Our family of origin also shapes us in ways known and unknown, both good and bad. Where we were raised shapes us by the power of that place, and any church we may attend appeals to divine authority to change us according to the will of God.

So back to the road to Emmaus with the two disciples. What unfolds is another experience of the ordinary turned extraordinary.

The two men think nothing of stopping at the appropriate time and sharing prayer and a meal together. What Jesus did was nothing but ordinary too. He took the bread they were going to eat anyway, said the prayer they would have also said had he not been there, and served it to the two men, all very usual. Except it was in this ordinary experience of table fellowship and prayer that the two recognized who had been with them all along.

I can imagine that many of us can strongly identify with this story, and that is why I am spending so much time on it. So much of our lives involve traveling here and there, going to work, checking emails, eating meals, and chatting with family and friends, all very ordinary things. But can we come to see the Risen Lord who journeys with us along the path of our lives? It might not be Emmaus exactly, but we are all journeying somewhere, and Christ the Lord is on the path alongside us.

You see, many people see Christ as a divisive religious figure, even in the religion of the Bible, and he is exactly the opposite. All of those who follow or place their faith and trust in Jesus are really just seeking God.

Just like the people of Israel in the Old Testament are taught to view themselves as those who have Abraham, Isaac, and Jacob as their patriarchs, as those who have been redeemed from slavery in Egypt. They are cared for by God in the wilderness, made a holy nation at Sinai, and led into the Promised Land.

People who follow Jesus Christ are the new Israel, the people of God formed by the story of Israel's Messiah. Called by Jesus to follow him, we walk with him among the poor and needy, we scratch our heads and try to figure out his teaching, we receive fish and bread from his hands and distribute it to the hungry, and we turn to him when the storm overwhelms our boat. In awe, we see him transfigured in glory on the Mount. When he stoops to wash our feet, we blush in shame. We sense impending doom in Gethsemane. We weep helplessly and feel all hope leave our hearts as he breathes his last on the cross. And then our mouths drop open in bewilderment, much like the disciples on the road to Emmaus when he appears alive and transformed among us.

And as we can see from the scriptures, Jesus was very adamant that, when you listened to what he said and did what he asked and followed him, you were really following God, as we can see in John 14:23–24, "Anyone who loves me will obey my teaching. My Father will love them, and we will come to them and make our home with them. Anyone who does not love me will not obey my teaching. These words you hear are not my own; they belong to the Father who sent me."

You can see in this quote from Jesus that the whole point of his coming was for God to bring himself into a closer relationship with us through a personal relationship with Jesus. These are really God's words speaking through Christ, and God is coming to you if you will obey the teachings of Jesus. We can see this confirmed further in John 5:36–37, "I have testimony weightier than that of John. For the works that the Father has given me to finish—the very works that I am doing—testify that the Father has sent me. And the Father who sent me has himself testified concerning me."

Jesus is saying here that God has sent him to finish what God started. These works include developing personal relationships with almost everyone he encounters and bringing about positive change in the lives of everyone to live a life more closely associated with God as a part of it. And you can see this through the relationship that Jesus himself has with God in John 8:29, "The one who sent me is with me; he has not left me alone, for I always do what pleases him."

You can see right here that God is with, beside, and working along with Jesus. It is a very personal, loving, and intimate relationship that God the Father has with Jesus, the Son. And that is exactly the same as Jesus who God sent and is trying to have a relationship with us.

Jesus has become like a bridge between us and this immense God so we can have a loving and tender relationship that is meant for us and to seek God as the ultimate person to lean on as we journey through life. Jesus tells us this in Matthew 11:28–30, "Come to me, all you who are weary and burdened, and I will give you rest. Take my yoke upon you and learn from me, for I am gentle and humble in heart, and you will find rest for your souls. For my yoke is easy and my burden is light."

But Jesus continues to make it known that, as we seek him, we are really seeking God. And as we look to this tender and loving Jesus to meet our needs, we are seeing God. Jesus confirms this in John 12:44–50,

> Then Jesus cried out, "Whoever believes in me does not believe in me only, but in the one who sent me. The one who looks at me is seeing the one who sent me. I have come into the world as a light, so that no one who believes in me should stay in darkness. If anyone hears my words but does not keep them, I do not judge that person. For I did not come to judge the world, but to save the world. There is a judge for the one who rejects me and does not accept my words; the very words I have spoken will condemn them at the last day. For I did not speak on my own, but the Father who sent me commanded me to say all that I have spoken. I know that his command leads to eternal life. So whatever I say is just what the Father has told me to say."

You may seek Jesus, look to him, and live by his teachings, and I would hope that you would become as Jesus is, "the light of the world. Whoever follows me will never walk in darkness, but will have the light of life." (John 8:12b)

This being true, there can be no mistake since Jesus himself in

John 12 referenced above that we are seeing God when looking at Jesus, "The one who looks at me is seeing the one who sent me." We must never forget this. When we come to Jesus, we are really coming to God. Even with the precious gift of salvation and eternal life that we have been given through Jesus, Jesus makes it plain for us to see and know that whatever we are following from Christ; we are still following God, "My sheep listen to my voice; I know them, and they follow me. I give them eternal life, and they shall never perish; no one will snatch them out of my hand. My Father, who has given them to me, is greater than all; no one can snatch them out of my Father's hand. I and the Father are one." (John 10:27–30)

It is very clear through most everything that Jesus says that, if you are seeking him, needing him, or relying on him, you are really coming to God. "I am the way and the truth and the life. No one comes to the Father except through me. If you really know me, you will know my Father as well." (John 14:6)

The statement "I am the good shepherd" that Jesus made in John 10:11 and again in John 10:14 was a teaching point that Jesus used in the lives of those around him. Throughout the history of the Jews, sheep have played an integral part in their economy. The sheep and other livestock determined a person's wealth. Not only was Jesus's use of the shepherd important in the present to illustrate the statement he was making, his use of the shepherd also points to the past. It was used in the Old Testament to express God's will in the lives of the Jews and for the whole world through his appointed good shepherd. The illustration also showed the deity of Christ, the goal of John in the writing of this gospel.

"I am the good shepherd" is set in a monologue that Jesus was using to share and teach the Pharisees and others who were in his presence. Unfortunately the Pharisees had just treated one of their own, the blind man that Jesus had healed, with "a prejudice that blinded them to anything but their own preconceived opinions." The purpose and meaning as it applied to Jesus's monologue was to show that, like a shepherd managing his flock, so does Jesus take care of his own. The people who will become his flock are the ones who can see and believe through faith, the ones who come through him to God. This is why Jesus came, to get people to seek him and, in that doing, seek or return to God.

Now the miracle of healing a blind man had just happened, and the Pharisees had questioned the man. When the Pharisees didn't like what they had heard, they decided to drive out the man from the temple. When Jesus heard, he came to the man and asked him in John 9:35, "Do you believe in the Son of Man?" The man asked who the Son was, and Jesus said it was him. Immediately the man professed his belief in the Son of Man.

Jesus then said in John 9:39, "For judgment I came into this world, that those who do not see may see, and those who see may become blind." Some Pharisees who were nearby heard and asked the question if they were blind as well. They asked this in confusion, even though they were the appointed leaders and teachers of Israel.

After answering them with "If you were blind ..." in John 9:41, Jesus started a monologue in John 10 with how he was the door and that those who did not use the door are like thieves and robbers that sneak over the wall to do harm, but only the shepherd can enter through the door. The sheep know the voice of the shepherd and follow him as he leads them from place to place, and the shepherd knows the name of the sheep and calls to them.

These are the next points that Jesus makes. The first part is about how he is the door of the sheepfold, and he expands into his "I am the good shepherd" in the second part of the monologue. Though the "good shepherd" is the stronger statement, the door plays a very important part in Jesus's speech.

Jesus illustrated the protection of the sheep with a narrow door to show that all the sheep (or flock) inside the fold would be protected from the thieves. The blind man healed in the previous chapter "is a member of the flock of the good shepherd," and what was true of him is true of the whole flock. This shows that, not only would the healed man be protected, all of God's people would be shielded as well. By Jesus stating this, he was making the claim that, like a door, he was the way into God's protection. In verse 10, he describes the thieves and robbers who would come not through the door but over the wall to do damage. In the same manner, Jesus is our door to God today, the same as it was then.

When the Pharisees failed to see the significance, he switched tactics and expanded on the theme. By stating in verse 11, "I am the good shepherd," Jesus changes from being in a protective role (the door) to a leadership role (the shepherd), and today he is still in the leadership role of the shepherd, shepherding us to God.

In the next few verses, Jesus explains how the shepherd would give his life for his sheep. There are several key points about the word "life" in this application. Not only would the shepherd give his life, he'd also give life to the sheep. Then he describes the hirelings who did not care for the sheep. He compares them to the Pharisees and scribes and how they do not care for the people. This was demonstrated by their treatment of the healed man.

The Pharisees should have understood either theme because, in the Old Testament, there are multiple references to the word "shepherd" and how it is used to illustrate God's response to the human nature of man. For example, David uses the word in several psalms, "The lord is my shepherd; I shall not want" (Psalm 23). Also as it is written in Psalm 28:9, "Oh, save your people and bless your heritage! Be their shepherd and carry them forever" to ask for needs to be met and protection of the people.

Specifically in Psalm 23, David is asking for the guidance of the Lord through the illustration of what a shepherd should do in the lives of the sheep, for example, to be the leader, to be the protector, and to come after lost sheep. The verse that captures this most strongly is Psalm 23:4 (KJV), "Yea, though I walk through the valley of the shadow of death, I will fear no evil: for thou art with me; thy rod and thy staff they comfort me."

Though the verses before and after this speak of what the shepherd does, this verse points to another Old Testament verse in Isaiah 40:11 (KJV), "He shall feed his flock like a shepherd: he shall gather the lambs with his arm, and carry them in his bosom, and shall gently lead those that are with young."

Hence, these scriptures and many others like them were a consistent theme throughout the Old Testament. Much like David and countless examples of people today, we can seek guidance from God through Jesus Christ.

In another example, we can compare and contrast the positive and negative aspects of the shepherd illustration. In Ezekiel 34, we are shown when the appointed shepherds (or hirelings) do wrong. Though there is more to the chapter, verse 10 (KJV) describes God's anger toward those shepherds who were appointed over his people, "Thus saith the Lord GOD; Behold, I am against the shepherds; and I will require my flock at their hand, and cause them to cease from feeding the flock; neither shall the shepherds feed themselves any more; for I will deliver my flock from their mouth, that they may not be meat for them."

The leaders of Israel had failed in their duties as the shepherds of God's people and would not be trusted anymore. God turns around and promises several things, a pledge to take care of the people, to have a separation of the fat and the lean, and the coming of the Messiah to fulfill God's promise by being the good shepherd. In the Old Testament, the leaders struggled with their responsibilities, just as the Pharisees and scribes were failing also in their responsibility in leading the people.

The deity of Christ is pointed out in the illustration around the phrase "I am the good shepherd." By giving his life to his sheep,

Jesus is reinforcing the fact that the cross was coming, even though the Pharisees and others did not understand that implication. By the sacrifice on the cross, Jesus, in love, promises eternal protection to his flock. The flock included more than just the Jews. It also included the Gentiles and essentially all of the world's people. This is reinforced in John 10:16 when Jesus promises to bring other sheep into the fold. The love that Jesus speaks from is the same love that John speaks of in the famous verse, 3:16, "For God so loved the world that he gave his only begotten Son …"

Through his Old Testament writers, God expressed a plan for a shepherd to come and take care of his people. When Jesus reaffirmed this with his "I am" statement, he stated the fact that he was in unity with his Father, which includes the ability to protect those who believe that Jesus is, just like the door, the only way to God.

Once the flock has gone through the door, Jesus, as the Good Shepherd, knows each one by name and leads them in love. Though he is the living Word, which was here from the beginning, he has left his Word and sent the Spirit to lead and protect his flock. So if only we will seek him, he will protect us as well.

One of the best things about Jesus Christ is there is no doubt, based on historical fact, that a man by the name of Jesus existed. Calendars declare the year AD 2015 (AD is Latin for *Anno Domini* or "year of our Lord." BC is "before Christ"), so time itself bears record of his existence, although some persons are trying to change those historical time frames to BCE and CE meaning "before the Common Era" and "Common Era," which are both meaningless.

But what specific function did Jesus have on this earth? Isaiah, the Old Testament prophet, well-respected and quoted often by many Jewish people, had this to say in Isaiah 61:1–2a around 750 BC,

> The Spirit of the Sovereign Lord is on me, because the
> Lord has anointed me to proclaim good news to the

poor. He has sent me to bind up the brokenhearted, to proclaim freedom for the captives and release from darkness for the prisoners, to proclaim the year of the LORD's favor.

This prophetic statement in 750 BC spoke of a time in the future when God's Holy Spirit would be upon someone. His Holy Spirit would anoint (which means "chosen one") to bring good news to the poor and to heal those who have broken hearts and no hope. This chosen one would proclaim a pardon to all who are prisoners of sin, and he would proclaim he was there to begin the year that God's favor would be upon all men and women.

When Jesus began his ministry, he came into the synagogue in his hometown of Nazareth. Now let's see what happened in the year AD 30.

He went to Nazareth, where he had been brought up, and on the Sabbath day he went into the synagogue, as was his custom. He stood up to read, and the scroll of the prophet Isaiah was handed to him. Unrolling it, he found the place where it is written: "The Spirit of the Lord is on me, because he has anointed me to proclaim good news to the poor. He has sent me to proclaim freedom for the prisoners and recovery of sight for the blind, to set the oppressed free, to proclaim the year of the Lord's favor." Then he rolled up the scroll, gave it back to the attendant and sat down. The eyes of everyone in the synagogue were fastened on him. He began by saying to them, "Today this scripture is fulfilled in your hearing." (Luke 4:16–21)

In other words, Jesus is saying that he is the one whom Isaiah had prophesied about. He is the anointed one. Of course everyone sitting there and witnessing this would naturally be skeptical and start looking at each other and saying to each other, "Isn't this Joseph's son?"

The congregation within the temple were obviously skeptical and questioning Jesus and thinking, "Wait a minute. You are just the son of Joseph, the carpenter. We know who you are. We have seen you grow up from this little boy to become a carpenter like your father, and now you are going to stand in front of us and proclaim you are the Savior of the world of whom our most respected prophet Isaiah spoke?"

And Jesus said to them, "Surely you will quote this proverb to me: 'Physician, heal yourself!' And you will tell me, 'Do here in your hometown what we have heard that you did in Capernaum.'" (Luke 4:23 KJV)

Jesus was prophesying that one day, over three and a half years from now, they would utter those words, "Physician, heal Thyself." And they mocked him by telling him to do all of the "signs and wonders" that he had demonstrated by God's authority, like Isaiah foretold, "but I say to you—No prophet is accepted in his own country." Matthew 13:58 says, "And he did not do many miracles there because of their lack of faith." Today is no different from that moment in history when Jesus came to deliver the message of why he came to earth, to preach the good news to the poor.

My understanding of what Jesus was saying is, "Those of you who have nothing, I come to bring good news that you can have everything, both now and here on this earth and later in the kingdom from where I came. And all you have to do is have faith in me and believe I am this one whom Isaiah told you about."

Jesus answered to the masses that were highly skeptical and doubting, "I am the way and the truth and the life. No one comes to the Father except through me. If you really know me, you will know my Father as well. From now on, you do know him and have seen him." (John 14:6–7)

Jesus exists because he came to preach or declare how those who were held captive by sin could be delivered from the condemnation of that iniquity, just as you and I can also be delivered from the sins that have a hold on us.

A part of Jesus's mission on earth was to teach all who are held captive by their sin and therefore condemned to spend an eternity in a place called the lake of fire could be set free. It would require simple faith and belief that the One who Isaiah and now Jesus said would come had in fact arrived.

Jesus declared he would also give sight to the blind, as Isaiah predicted, but Jesus would give sight physically to the blind while preaching that he would also give sight spiritually to all whom Satan blinded, so they too could see how they can be forgiven of their sins and set free from the condemnation of sin under the law of Moses.

Jesus wrapped up why he exists to all those who would listen, "The Spirit of the Lord is on me, because he has anointed me to proclaim good news to the poor. He has sent me to proclaim freedom for the prisoners and recovery of sight for the blind, to set the oppressed free, to proclaim the year of the Lord's favor." (Luke 4:18–19)

Jesus was foretelling how he would be the one who would be able to set them free from condemnation of sin. He would do this by dying on a cross for the sins of all mankind, and he told of how they could be set free.

The good news was that, if they had faith in this Christ, this Savior of mankind, and if they believed he is whom Isaiah predicted would come, the Son of God, they could be free indeed.

My understanding from John 10:10 is that the thief (Satan) comes only to steal (meaning to steal your ability to gain heaven), to kill (meaning to ensure you die a spiritual death, which is eternal separation from God in the same place that Satan will end up, the lake of fire), and to destroy. And Jesus came so these same people whom Satan wants to destroy might have life (meaning eternal life in heaven) and they might have it more abundantly (a better life here on the earth).

This is why Jesus came to the earth. This is why he exists, and this same message and mission prevails today, as much as it did when Jesus preached the good news back in the time he physically walked this earth.

Jesus knew then—and he knows now—that people will constantly struggle to wrap their brains and hearts around his message and his mission or to listen to Satan, the great deceiver who wants only to destroy and prevent anyone from gaining access into heaven.

It's all about choices. Through the Holy Spirit, God always points people to Jesus, who directs people to God. God said in John 6:40, "For my Father's will is that everyone who looks to the Son, and believes in him, shall have everlasting life, and I will raise them up at the last day."

The most famous verse in the Bible is John 3:16 (KJV), "For God so loved the world, that he gave his only begotten Son, that whosoever believeth in him should not perish, but have Everlasting life." Jesus's existence, therefore, should be crystal clear. He was sent by God, chosen or anointed to do all that Isaiah and Jesus said he would do.

The Jewish people, who adore and respect the writings of the great prophet Isaiah, should recall these words,

> In the past he humbled the land of Zebulun and the land of Naphtali, but in the future he will honor Galilee of the nations, by the way of the Sea, beyond the Jordan— The people walking in darkness have seen a great light; on those living in the land of deep darkness a light has dawned." (Isaiah 9:1b–2)

Right after that, Isaiah prophesied that something would come to pass in the future. An "anointed one" would come to Galilee, land of Gentiles, and all who live in darkness (sinful state) will see the "light." And to those people who live in the darkness of sin, therefore under the shadow of the punishment of eternal death or separation from God, this light of the world will spring forth. This "deliverer" will come.

In Isaiah 9:6–7, Isaiah prophesied,

> For a child is born to us, a son is given to us. The government will rest on his shoulders. And he will be called Wonderful Counselor, Mighty God, Everlasting Father, Prince of Peace. His government and its peace will never end. He will reign on David's throne and over his kingdom, establishing and upholding it with justice and righteousness from that time and forever. The zeal of the Lord Almighty will accomplish this.

Isaiah predicted that one day in the future a child would be born, and this child would be called Prince of Peace and would rule his own government. And there would be peace on the earth. And he would be called God, part of the Trinity.

This prophecy said there would be a Messiah. All of this happened when a baby was born in a manger in the little town of Bethlehem, also predicted as the place this Messiah would be born.

The prophet Micah said in Micah 5:2 (KJV), "But thou, Bethlehem Ephratah, though thou be little among the thousands of Judah, yet out of thee shall he come forth unto me that is to be ruler in Israel; whose goings forth have been from of old, from everlasting."

The same God of old from eternity past is the same God who will be ruler over Israel in the future through his Son, a babe to be born in the city of Bethlehem. And Micah wrote this around 750 BC, but it happened just the way God spoke it through his prophets.

How people can believe that all of the prophecies of the Old

Testament that came true when Jesus arrived were nothing more than a coincidence is beyond me. They stake their eternal destiny on believing a lie from Satan, the one who wants people to die in their sinful state and end up in the lake of fire with him.

In Matthew 5:16 (NKJV), Jesus said we have a job to do for him when he goes back to heaven, to "let your light so shine before others, that they may see your good deeds, and glorify your Father in heaven."

Are we letting our light, which is our salvation and relationship with God through his Son Jesus, shine so others whom we know can see it? Or are we hiding it? If so, why are we hiding it? Are we ashamed to know Christ? Jesus said, "If you deny me before men on earth, I will deny you before my Father who is in Heaven." (Matthew 10:30 NKJV) Jesus also declared, "Think not that I am come to destroy the law, or the prophets: I am not come to destroy the Law but to fulfill. For verily I say unto you, till heaven and earth pass, one jot or one tittle shall in no wise pass from the law, till all be fulfilled." (Matthew 5:17–18 KJV)

My understanding of what Jesus was saying is that the law will be used to judge all who have rejected him and what he did on the cross to save them from the punishment of breaking the laws of God. The same law of Moses will be used to judge those who reject Jesus as Lord and Savior. So those who live by the law shall also be punished by the law.

Instead Jesus died on the cross to take your sins and my sins upon himself. He is willing to exchange his righteousness for our sin, if we call upon his name in belief that he is the Messiah, the Son of God, and the only one who can forgive us of our sins because he is the only one who has paid for them on that cross.

Jesus cautions us as followers, "Whosoever therefore shall break one of these least commandments, and shall teach men so, he shall be called the least in the kingdom of heaven: but whosoever shall do and teach them, the same shall be called great in the kingdom of heaven." (Matthew 5:19 KJV)

Whoever of his followers breaks those laws and teaches men to also violate those commandments (through our actions or words) will get into heaven all right, but they will be the very least in heaven. And those who do his commandments and teach them to others (through actions, deeds, or words) shall be rewarded greatly in heaven.

Jesus continues, "For I say unto you, that except your righteousness shall exceed the righteousness of the scribes and Pharisees, ye shall in no case enter into the kingdom of heaven." (Matthew 5:20 KJV) In other words, without being righteous or without sin, nobody can enter into the kingdom of God, heaven.

There is only one way to become righteous so that God can see you and hear your prayers, and that is by receiving the "cloak of righteousness" that Jesus offers to all who receive him as Lord and Savior. That "cloak of righteousness" covers us and our sin so God can see us and hear our prayers.

Matthew 4:23–25 (KJV) says,

> And Jesus went about all Galilee, teaching in their synagogues, and preaching the gospel of the kingdom, and healing all manner of sickness and all manner of disease among the people. And his fame went throughout all Syria: and they brought unto him all sick people that were taken with diverse diseases and torments, and those which were possessed with devils, and those which were lunatic, and those that had the palsy; and he healed them. And there followed him great multitudes of people from Galilee, and from Decapolis, and from Jerusalem, and from Judea, and from beyond Jordan.

When Jesus was here on the earth, he did many signs, wonders, and miracles. And historians do not deny any of that. Now some two thousand years later, we have read the history, and yet people still deny that Jesus even existed. How foolish not to believe reports from historical facts.

This reminds me of the story of lepers. Leprosy was a dreaded disease back in the time of Christ. They would have to stay clear of people and wave their hands, motioning people to steer clear. And they were forced to yell, "Unclean! Unclean!" Nobody would come near them.

We are "unclean" or unrighteous today, and yet Jesus wants to come to us to heal us of our sin, just like he physically touched the untouchable lepers in the day. Matthew 8:1–3 (NKJV) tells us that history,

> When He had come down from the mountain, great multitudes followed Him, and behold, a leper came and worshiped Him, saying, Lord, if You are willing, You can make me clean. Then Jesus put out His hand and touched him, saying, I am willing: be cleansed. Immediately his leprosy was cleansed.

Jesus wants to touch you today—the untouchables, the unclean, the sinner. All you have to do is have the same faith that the leper had, "Jesus, if you want to, you can cleanse me of all my sins. I believe you are the Messiah, the Son of God, and you died for my sins that day when you went to the cross. I believe that you can forgive my sins and cleanse me from all of them, and I am asking (just like that leper did) that you will cleanse me, save my soul, and give me your cloak of righteousness so that God can see me and hear my prayers."

We are like caterpillars. They crawl around in a low fashion, hugging the ground and trying to slowly get by obstacles on the ground. Eventually they make it to a tree, climb a limb, and form a cocoon. Over time, what emerges is a beautiful butterfly, who can now soar above all those obstacles that took it so long to pass when it was crawling. Is it time for you to take flight, to soar the way God intended for you to?

The prophet Isaiah said in Isaiah 40:31 (KJV), "But they that wait upon the LORD shall renew their strength; they shall mount up with wings as eagles; they shall run, and not be weary; and they shall walk, and not faint."

You have choices to make now:

1. Accept all that Jesus has to offer you, including eternal life in heaven with him through salvation, or reject him and spend your eternal destiny in the lake of fire.
2. Once you accept Jesus as Lord and Savior, drift through life with a ticket to heaven in your hand or always wonder what your life could have been had you asked God to show you what his plan and purpose is for your life.

I asked God to show me his plan and purpose for my life, and he has done all I asked. I have all he promised—peace, joy, patience, love for my fellow man, and no stress whatsoever—because Jesus told me not to take one thought for tomorrow but to only ask for what I need today. And God has shown me what my mission is while I am here on the planet. You can never know what could have been until you ask God to show you his plan and purpose for your life. Then once he delivers, you will be so happy that you asked him to do that for you.

Okay, so we have seen that there are plenty of examples that Jesus has changed lives and the paths that lives were on, but why should we trust in Jesus? What makes him so special? Well, the deity of Jesus Christ is the bedrock of biblical Christianity and a teaching found throughout the pages of the New Testament. If Jesus is God, then he has all authority in heaven and on earth.

Now what evidence do we have in scripture for the divine authority of Christ? In Mark 1:16–28, we have two scenes that demonstrate the sovereignty of the Messiah. In verses 16–20, we see Jesus exercise his authority over people. He encounters Peter, Andrew, James, and John while they are fishing on the Sea of Galilee. Jesus says, "Come, follow me, and I will make you fishers of men." (Mark 1:17). All four men literally and willingly drop everything and obey Jesus's command. And they do so immediately. "At once they left their nets and followed him." (Mark 1:18).

Now I'm sure you are thinking that this means nothing. So Jesus Christ is a charismatic guy. So are most people who attract other people and crowds when they speak. That's true, but it's not so much that they followed Jesus, but what they witnessed when following him makes it plain who Jesus is. And it also shows what Jesus is here to do for those who follow him, which I will explain further ahead.

In Mark 1:21–28, we see Jesus and his four disciples going to the synagogue in Capernaum on the Sabbath, where Jesus begins to teach those in attendance at the weekly worship service. A man is present who is demon-possessed. Demons know who Jesus is (God in a human body), and so are terrified by Jesus, fearful that Judgment Day has come.

So the man begins to yell at Jesus, which prompts Jesus to tell the demon to shut up and come out of the man. The demon does exactly what Jesus tells him to do. "The evil spirit shook the man violently and came out of him with a shriek." (Mark 1:26)

What can we learn about Jesus from these two scenes? That Jesus has authority over all. In both cases, Jesus issues commands that are obeyed. He is demonstrating his divine authority as the Son of God, and both human beings (the four fisherman) and superhuman beings (the demon) are subject to his authority. Jesus has the power to rule over all. He is the Christ, the long-awaited king prophesied about in the Old Testament who would come to establish his reign in the hearts of his people and over the forces of darkness.

Jesus also has compassion for all. Yet Jesus is a king filled with love for his subjects. In both cases, compassion motivates the commands to "Come, follow me" and "Come out of him." He has empathy for these four fisherman. By following him, their lives will be radically changed for the better. They are leaving their jobs as fisherman to enter a new calling, as not only disciples but apostles of King Jesus. Their decision to follow Jesus will not be easy to live out, but it will prove worthwhile beyond their wildest dreams, both in this life and in the one to come. This is where you and I have likely come to many times. We know the road to follow Jesus will not be easy, as evidenced by his life, which was not easy. The lives of the apostles who followed him were not easy and, in some cases, downright miserable.

But the gift of everlasting life given through him and the works of those who have followed him, even to this day, have spread throughout the world to have positive effects on the lives of millions throughout the world in the name of Jesus. We can see this from John 15:18–19, "If the world hates you, keep in mind that it hated me first. If you belonged to the world, it would love you as its own. As it is, you do not belong to the world, but I have chosen you out of the world. That is why the world hates you."

Likewise, compassion for the demon-possessed man motivated Jesus's command to the demon. His life was no doubt a miserable one. He had been a slave to the demon's every evil desire. Demons come to destroy life. And now in the blink of an eye, Jesus transformed this man's life. He was no longer in bondage to the forces of darkness. He was set free to serve the one who liberated him!

God sent Jesus here to do the same for us, to liberate us as well as those who are in the scriptures. And we have the chance to be liberated if we seek Jesus in word and counsel. It has been proven over and over that seeking Jesus even today has changed lives and relationships; caused physical, emotional, and mental healing; and made people risk their own lives to make lives better for others through their own work and charity. It has resulted in the transmitting or translating of the words and actions of Jesus Christ that they have read and experienced to improve the lives of other people, groups, and nations.

Oh, that we would realize the truth that, when Jesus issues a command for us to obey, he does so with our best interest in mind. Jesus's authority will be obeyed by all eventually and ultimately. We should also remember that Jesus is also known as the Great Comforter by verses such as this, "Come to me, all you who are weary and burdened, and I will give you rest. Take my yoke upon you and learn from me, for I am gentle and humble in heart, and you will find rest for your souls. For my yoke is easy and my burden is light." (Matthew 11:28–30).

These two episodes describe actual events. They are also pictures of the fate of every person. Like the four disciples, we can willingly submit to Jesus's authority as God in this life by exercising faith in him as our Lord, our Savior, and our Treasure. To do so is to align ourselves with God's will and thereby enter the kingdom of heaven. This is no easy decision to make or to implement, but it will be rewarded greatly both in this life and the next.

Whether in this life or the next, Paul's words will eventually come to pass, "At the name of Jesus every knee should bow ... and every tongue confess that Jesus is Lord." (Philippians 2:10–11)

chapter 7
Returning to God

greall great example we all know well to help us see how we can return to God and complete the circle that God began with each of us when we were born and he gave us life is to look to the *Wizard of Oz*.

One day Dorothy and Toto found themselves in a wondrous world not in Kansas anymore! For sure. You might say they arrived there by grace alone. In the midst of their mostly tranquil but unsatisfying life, an existence that had prompted Dorothy to dream of a better land "over the rainbow," they found that land solely through a power greater than themselves. A twister blew off the Plains, picked them up and twirled them 'round, and set them down in a new realm. Sepia tones turned to Technicolor, drab became dynamic, and everything was new. For the first time in her life, Dorothy felt alive. However, also for the first time, she knew that her ultimate dream was to find home. How could she find her way home?

Dorothy received a simple answer, "Follow the Yellow Brick Road." And looking up, she beheld a clear path of golden bricks winding around and leading off into the distance. This road, she was promised, would take her to the city of Oz, where she would meet the powerful Wizard of Oz. He would give her the answer and show her the way to go home. The advice she got, of course, proved inadequate. Following the Yellow Brick Road made things worse and ultimately left her stranded and still wondering how she would ever get home.

It must be admitted that Dorothy found blessings and learned lessons along the way. She found friends as needy as she, who joined her on the quest to find answers at the end of the road. She also found danger and difficulty. Various troubles and obstacles hindered and threatened the journey.

In confronting them, this humble farm girl discovered hidden resources within herself, as well as the reassurance and security that comes from having loyal companions to help her fight her battles. Dorothy also learned that the world has its charlatans, who, despite their public reputations, are nothing more than pathetic imposters. They influence others through the power of suggestion and manipulation. They know how to market themselves. They build great cities but hide behind little curtains.

When it was all over and she had reached the end of the road, Dorothy stood with Toto in her arms and a tear in her eye. She had not found the way home. The Yellow Brick Road, as simple and well-marked as it was, had led her nowhere. The great city had proven no better than the farmyard at satisfying her heart. Her friends couldn't give her what she ultimately needed. Nor could the great and powerful Wizard of Oz.

Having begun her journey by the gracious intervention of a power greater than herself, she now realized that all the paths she had taken subsequently were dead ends. Though they came highly recommended and were firmly believed by those who promoted them, they could not ultimately help Dorothy or lead her home.

In the end, however, grace once more intervened. As Dorothy stood weeping, Glinda the Good Witch appeared.

> Dorothy: Oh, will you help me? Can you help me?
> Glinda: You don't need to be helped any longer. You've always had the power to go back to Kansas.
> Dorothy: I have?

Scarecrow: Then why didn't you tell her before?
Glinda: Because she wouldn't have believed me. She
had to learn it for herself.

What? Read those words again, "You've always had the power to
go back to Kansas." From the moment grace set her down in a new
land, she had the power to find home, the ability to make the journey,
and the resources to make it all the way. She didn't know it then, but
it had all been given to her.

She didn't need the Yellow Brick Road, the city, or the Wizard
of Oz. She and her friends (who by the way learned the same lesson)
didn't require what they or others thought they needed. All the paths
laid out for them proved to be worthless. All the experts proved
incapable of granting their deepest needs and wants. They only needed
to make the journey. In walking, they found the way. I now refer you
to Galatians 3:2–4 (The Message),

> Let me put this question to you: How did your new
> life begin? Was it by working your heads off to please
> God? Or was it by responding to God's Message to
> you? Are you going to continue this craziness? For
> only crazy people would think they could complete
> by their own efforts what was begun by God. If you
> weren't smart enough or strong enough to begin it,
> how do you suppose you could perfect it? Did you
> go through this whole painful learning process for
> nothing? It is not yet a total loss, but it certainly will
> be if you keep this up!

You need not be making drastic lifestyle changes, joining this
movement or that organization, or digging a pit and spending several
hours a day praying and fasting in it. (And yes, there were monks who

actually did this because they felt they were so unworthy of God. They had to live in a pit, and these were monks.)

No, let me repeat from Matthew 11:28–30, "Come to me, all you who are weary and burdened, and I will give you rest. Take my yoke upon you and learn from me, for I am gentle and humble in heart, and you will find rest for your souls. For my yoke is easy and my burden is light."

God through Jesus Christ is already here waiting on you, ahead of you, and next to you, hoping you will continue to take steps toward him and the best life you could imagine, as it is the life God had planned for you. Is God going to grant you this change tomorrow? No. But over time it will happen.

If we are working to find God or make him a part of our lives and are not doing things that will take us further from God, we will find him, and he will become a part of our lives. You can see this in Proverbs 8:17, "I love those who love me, and those who seek me find me."

We need only to look at the apostle Paul to see that God was working throughout his life to bring him into the life God had planned for him. Did Paul change completely overnight? No, but over the course of his life, including his Christian life, God was perfectly patient with him.

Your small baby steps in this life are nothing to talk about. What's really interesting is what you will become as you find what God has planned for you. I would challenge you, "Ask and seek what he wants for your life." You just might be amazed to find your journey was a circle to God and God was with you the whole time, just like he was with the apostle Paul.